# Writing for All

Sylvia Edwards

David Fulton Publishers
London

David Fulton Publishers Ltd
Ormond House, 26-27 Boswell Street, London WC1N 3JD

First published in Great Britain by David Fulton Publishers 1999



*British Library Cataloguing in Publication Data*
A catalogue record for this book is available from the British Library

ISBN 1-85346-602-6



Typeset by Jane Plowman, Leighton Buzzard
Printed in Great Britain by Bell and Bain Ltd, Glasgow

# Contents

# Acknowledgements

The author wishes to thank colleagues in Oldham, Lancashire, Hull and, in particular, those in the East Riding of Yorkshire, from whom information and many examples of good practice in developing writing have originated and made this book possible.

# Introduction

Writing is part of literacy. It is also part of the National Literacy Strategy (NLS) drive towards raising standards. Literacy operates as a currency and value judgement throughout society, and an illiteracy label carries negative implications for a person's work and social life.

In schools, reading has traditionally received more attention than writing, with the result that many children struggle into adulthood still unable to write effectively, with their self-esteem damaged by the experience of trying to become skilled writers, and their perceived failure.

The NLS Framework for Teaching (DfEE 1998) provided a structure for reading and writing in order to promote literacy for all; by setting out the structure for reading and writing together, the Framework recognises their interdependence.

This book considers writing through the context of the NLS and its philosophy of inclusion, exploring the NLS writing objectives as programmes of study for all learners and relating these to the National Curriculum levels through which writing competency is assessed.

Chapter 1 reflects on writing as communication, the essential starting point to exploring writing skills and strategies: how do good writers write? How can all learners become writers? It focuses on those who struggle to write: what are their writing difficulties and how can they be eradicated or reduced?

*Writing for All* is a practical manual. Its aim is to enable all teachers to approach the teaching of writing with confidence and to promote success for all children in the classroom. Written for teachers in mainstream and special schools who aspire to raise standards in writing, it contains a wealth of practical advice and information to help schools achieve this. *Writing for All* will help teachers to:

- promote pupils' confidence in writing;
- promote life-long writers;
- raise writing standards for all children; and
- enable a maximum number of children to attain National Curriculum Level 4 or above in writing.

This book also addresses the following key issues, in the context of the NLS:

- what is an effective writer and how can we enable more children to achieve as writers?
- what should a policy of 'writing for all' contain?
- how can we make the best use of human and material resources in order to raise writing standards?
- how can the assessment and recording of pupils' writing inform good policy and practice for the benefit of all learners?

*Chapter 1*

# Writing as Communication

## *Why do writers write?*

Writing communicates messages. Consider the following examples: shopping lists, formal letters (to bank manager), reports, lesson plans, daily diary, rough notes to milkman or family, memos for work, postcards, notices, letters to friends, Christmas or greetings cards, application forms, novels, articles for a magazine, theses, minutes of a staff meeting.

These examples illustrate a proportion of adult writing, most of which is done without thinking about the skills and strategies which control the activity. Mature writers communicate almost as easily through writing as they do through speech, expressing emotions, intentions and actions according to their purpose for writing and their intended audience.

## *What is writing?*

The range of adult writing illustrates why writers write, but to address difficulties we must know what writing involves.

### Word level

At word level the writer may need to consider:

- letter formation;
- the correct placing of letters in relation to line;
- spelling of words; and
- spacing between words.

### Sentence level

At its simplest, writing at sentence level requires:

- knowledge of how words make up sentences;
- punctuation skills; and
- knowledge of when to use upper and lower case letters.

### Text level

The writer builds on word and sentence knowledge to:

- group sentences into a paragraph;
- sequence paragraphs into text, often with sub-sections;
- structure headings and signposts for the reader;
- use purpose, function and audience to shape the style and presentation of the final piece; and
- consider sentences and words as part of the whole text.

## *Purpose, function and audience*

All writing has purpose. For example, a note to the milkman results in more milk delivered, or a letter to the bank manager may result in the requested loan. The purpose of this book is to support improved standards in writing for all children.

Writing also has different functions: the note to a son or spouse may be to inform of your whereabouts and when you will return; the letter to the bank manager may be to request financial support; the function of a novel is usually to entertain; the shopping list is a memory aid. The purpose and the function of writing depend upon the writer's audience: a diary is written for the writer himself, while a report may be written for colleagues to consider, and a crime novel will be written for mass readership. The audience will affect the formal or informal style of the writing, though the form may be the same. For example, a letter to a friend is written differently from a letter to the local Member of Parliament.

The style and presentation of a piece of writing depends upon all of the points raised above. As long as you can read the scribbles of your own diary and arrive at the right place at the right time, it hardly matters about neatness. On the other hand, a job application requires precise content and immaculate presentation.

## Writing in school

Consider the points raised so far:

- purpose;
- function;
- audience; and
- style and level of formality.

All writing should have the above attributes, but the need to do some writing every day may detract from its real purpose and function. It is easy to lose track of why children need to write if the activity itself masks the reality. Writing may appear unclear to children – they may be asked to simply draw a picture and write about it; while in science they are required to write up an experiment, and in history they may have to answer questions from a textbook. Lack of instruction on different forms of writing is often reflected by poor results.

How real is the school-based audience? Much writing in school tends to be for the teacher. To 'write a story' without a real readership does little to motivate learners and promotes a message that writing is an assessment exercise, rather than a process towards genuine production. School writing rarely considers the function of the outcome: how often are children explicitly taught how to report, explain, request, describe or instruct effectively through writing?

Consider the presentation of school writing. How often do we ask children to copy out written work which could be left as it is? Writing for ourselves, as an aid to memory and organisation, has no need for presentation. All children, especially those with special educational needs (SEN), need to know when presentation is important and when it is not, to allow their thinking to focus on other essential elements of the writing process.

Writing for a real purpose to a genuine audience may involve children in:

- writing labels for the classroom cupboards/display;
- writing letters to the community, inviting real replies;
- advertising the school Christmas fair;
- writing book reviews for each other to read;
- writing stories for younger children and 'publishing' them;
- writing stories or poems for sharing in the literacy hour;
- contributing to the recording of their own progress;
- writing cards and messages for each other; or
- making notes as part of cross-curricular topic work, to be read and considered by the group.

As Baker (1995) reminds us, 'real writers learn to write by writing'.

## Writing in the NLS

The NLS Framework (DfEE 1998) strengthens the recognition that writing relates to reading. In practice, most reading and writing tasks occur together, yet each must be assessed separately in order to respond to writing difficulties. Children need to know that reading and writing are two sides of the same literacy coin, and that each enriches the other.

The NLS Framework (DfEE 1998) strengthens this view by stating, 'The context of pupils' reading, i.e. the texts, gives structures, themes and purposes for much of their writing . . . Pupils need to understand from an early stage that much of their writing will be read by other people and therefore needs to be accurate, legible and set out in an appropriate way.'

### NLS objectives

At word and sentence level, the objectives from the NLS Framework can be more easily measured and assessed. Consider the following objectives:

- spell common irregular words from Appendix List 1 (Year 1);
- ensure consistency in size and proportions of letters and the spacing between letters and words (Year 3);
- to use the term 'synonym' (Year 3);
- use word banks and dictionaries (Year 4);
- use known spellings as a basis for spelling other words with similar patterns or related meanings (Year 5); and
- identify mis-spelt words in own writing . . . (Year 6).

It is easy to observe how far the above objectives have been achieved. Similarly, NLS word and sentence level objectives can easily reflect targets for writing as stated on Individual Educational Plans (IEPs) for children with SEN. By contrast, many NLS objectives for writing composition are as programmes of study, supporting the process towards writing competence. They are staging points, each helping to build the skills and strategies a learner writer needs to eventually achieve at National Curriculum Level 4 or above.

Consider these NLS objectives for writing composition:

- write labels for drawings and diagrams (Year 1);
- write simple instructions (Year 2);
- use story settings from reading, e.g. re-describe, use in own writing, write a different story in the same setting (Year 2);
- write a non-chronological report . . . (Year 4);
- draft . . . individual . . . letters for real purposes (Year 5);
- write a brief synopsis of a text . . . (Year 6).

Clearly, many objectives for writing composition may need to be focused to reflect writing targets for pupils with SEN. A child may 'write an extended story worked on over time on a theme identified in reading'. A learner can achieve his objective without having developed his writing competence.

If spelling, handwriting or sentence structure is not accessible to the reader, written work fails to communicate, yet we need to recognise the achievement of having written an extended story in the first place – the imagination of the writer may be brilliant. The point of these reflections is simply to analyse the implications of the NLS objectives for the teaching and learning of writing. We need to recognise the NLS achievement yet at the same time develop the skills and strategies of all writers towards maturity.

## Writing in the National Curriculum

While NLS objectives form the context of learning to write, the National Curriculum level descriptions state the criteria by which writing competence will be assessed. The general requirements for English at all Key Stages of the National Curriculum (DfE 1995) state that, for pupils to develop as effective writers, they should be taught to use:

- compositional skills – developing ideas and communicating meaning to a reader, using a wide-ranging vocabulary and an effective style, organising and structuring sentences grammatically, and whole texts coherently;
- presentational skills – accurate punctuation, correct spellings and legible handwriting; and
- a widening variety of forms for different purposes.

The effective writer needs to combine all three elements in order to communicate. The central theme of this book is how to enable all children to acquire the skills of effective writing.

## *Differences between speaking and writing*

To a large extent, writing relies on the ability to place words and sentences together appropriately, reflecting spoken language. Writing to standard English requirements reflects an oral knowledge of standard English which can be brought into use as necessary, though speakers may use a different form of language among friends and family. The National Curriculum for English (DfE 1995) states, 'Differences between spoken and written forms relate to the spontaneity of speech and to its function in conversation, whereas writing is more permanent, often carefully crafted, and less dependent upon immediate responses.'

The crafting of writing is essential to the learning process. Many learners, particularly those who fail, are unaware of the stages through which some written work must progress before reaching the final version. On the other hand, much time is wasted if final versions or 'fair copies' are laboriously produced for no reason other than assessment.

## *Achieving balance*

If writing is accepted as a craft, the purpose behind the 'emergent writing' approach requires consideration. The NLS philosophy is for writing to be taught explicitly. Teachers are to model, guide, observe and coach learners towards maturity. There is a freshness to the writing experience. Yet writing is a hierarchical structure and can only be developed from what a child knows already: cursive writing cannot be acquired until a child forms letters correctly; paragraphs cannot be produced until a child forms sentences; and the spelling of multi-syllabic words cannot be acquired until a child spells simple words. Children with learning difficulties may learn to hate writing if they are asked to do what they are not yet ready for, and may mentally switch off from the writing experience because it is a painful reminder of their failure.

The theme of the NLS is that children with SEN need to be 'held in' to the learning process and helped to keep up with the majority, yet children cannot be expected to perform written tasks that are beyond their capabilities. Writing for all is achieved through a careful balance of what has to be taught and what children are ready to learn.

## *Establishing writing goals*

Few people aspire to be professional writers, yet many professions require skilful writing as a competency. Goals for learners must reflect the range of writing: achievement of NLS objectives by Year 6 is a mere staging point in the preparation for a lifetime of writing. Children also need to appreciate the pleasures of writing. If enjoyment is to be a goal, then children with SEN must retain their confidence that whatever they write, as their personal best, is respected and valued.

This chapter has presented writing as a communicative process, a reflection of speech; yet with a specific identity. Most writing activities are carefully crafted in relation to their purpose, function and audience for which they are written, even at word level; for example, writing labels on cupboards may involve decisions about upper or lower case lettering and their size. Children need to appreciate why some writing needs to be carefully presented while other forms can be left in a rough state. For many children with learning difficulties, this may be a key factor in motivating them to put pen to paper.

Children with learning difficulties need time to communicate through writing: poor writers gain confidence in an atmosphere of accepting trial and error. Learning to write takes place when there is no such thing as a wrong spelling or an incorrectly constructed sentence. Words and sentences are always 'somewhere along the road to rightness'.

The NLS Framework is based on the principle of high expectations for all learners. The writing objectives stated are challenging for children with SEN, yet the Framework itself provides scope for revisiting and consolidation. If all pupils are to communicate effectively through their writing:

> Their attainment needs to be carefully assessed so that pupils who have not achieved this basic standard can revise and consolidate Key Stage 1 work. Throughout Year 3 pupils may still need to cover or reinforce the word level objectives from Key Stage 1. There are objectives in the word level column in Year 3 and again in Year 4 to remind teachers of this. (NLS Framework for Teaching, DfEE 1998.)

The NLS recognises that, for many children, effective communication through writing will happen only as a result of continued reinforcement of taught skills, accompanied by a careful analysis of their writing difficulties.

*Chapter 2*

# Addressing Writing Difficulties

To address writing difficulties, teachers need to know what they are and how they are caused. The struggling writer is overwhelmed by an insurmountable barrier, and it is up to schools to unravel the complex reasons why learners struggle to write, and to address them.

## *What are writing difficulties?*

Bentley (1998) analyses writing problems under the headings of surface, content and process. Figure 2.1 lists some reasons why children struggle to write.

| | |
|---|---|
| **Surface problems** | poor pencil control<br>poor letter formation<br>chronically slow writing<br>poor spelling<br>poor layout and organisation |
| **Content problems** | unable to think of what to write<br>writes very little<br>work always unfinished<br>muddled organisation<br>repetitive stereotyped ideas |
| **Process problems** | has no desire to write<br>writes whole text when asked to draft<br>reluctant to revise writing<br>finds it hard to read own work<br>sees writing as handwriting and spelling<br>little sense of purpose or audience<br>is frustrated when writing is not perfect |

**Figure 2.1** Writing problems

The nature of writing difficulties is complex, and most children with problems will have been placed on the school SEN register at the appropriate stage. The following case studies show a range of writing difficulties. The IEP targets later in the chapter state the steps taken to address them.

### Case studies

*Anna*

Anna is in Year 2, at Stage 1 of the SEN Code of Practice. She appears to enjoy writing and shows no reluctance. Anna's main problem is spelling: many high frequency words are mis-spelt; upper and lower case letters are confused, with capitals sprinkled liberally within sentences, and words are often missed out. However, Anna has a good sense of space and letters are well placed. Figure 2.2 shows a sample of Anna's writing.

I hav sister a to Bruthers.
I hav Dog cold Sandy. My Dog
cums Wiv us. He dusnt lak it in car.

**Figure 2.2** Sample of Anna's writing

*Alan*

Alan is Year 5, at Stage 3 of the Code of Practice. Alan says he hates writing. His spelling is poor, but his handwriting is particularly weak. Alan produces very little of his own composition. What he does write is mainly copied. Figure 2.3 shows a sample of Alan's writing.

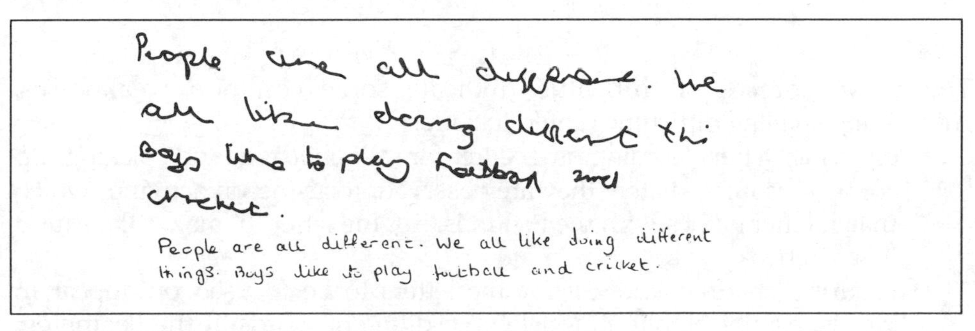


**Figure 2.3** Sample of Alan's writing

*Darren*

Darren is in Year 4, at Stage 5 of the Code of Practice. Darren's handwriting is perfect, and he delights in presenting neat work. He has perfected the art of asking friends for spellings, subversively copying or asking the teacher in order to avoid writing himself. Neatness has become an obsession with him. Darren will not put pen to paper without copying. Thus, few of the skills of writing are secure, apart from handwriting. For Darren, there is no process: his only outcome is to see a piece of writing without mistakes or amendments. Darren will not attempt to read his writing.

*What do the case studies illustrate?*

The three examples are real but the names have been changed. The examples illustrate the need to explore carefully writing difficulties in order to overcome them. Alan and Darren are both reluctant to write, while Anna writes happily almost without bothering about her inaccuracies.

Darren's example illustrates the need to look beneath the writing to observe the process as well as the production. I came across Darren in Year 4 and was amazed at the strategies he had acquired in order to avoid writing from what was in his own head: he had few spelling skills, still confused most letters, and could not place words together himself, although he could dictate them to an adult. Clearly, over-copying had allowed him to avoid writing rather than address his problems and resolve them.

## *Addressing writing difficulties*

The above case studies represent a large proportion of pupils whose writing difficulties often strangle motivation and act as a barrier to independent learning.

## Spelling difficulties

These may be demonstrated in the following ways:

- confusing letters which are similar in shape and/or orientation, or small details. Examples could be:
  - 'b', 'd' and 'p' differ only in orientation as do 'f' and 't';
  - the printed 'a', 'o' and 'c' differ in small details;
  - 'y' and 'g' are similar in shape; and
  - 'e' and 'c' appear the same if the 'e' is carelessly written;
- spelling phonetically, e.g. 'woz' for was, 'thay' for they;
- over- or under-use of phonic rules, e.g. 'cherrys';
- making the wrong choice when a selection of graphemes can match one phoneme, e.g. 'peech' for peach;
- poor visual memory; or
- reversals of letters in words, e.g. 'siad' for said.

*Solutions*

The above sources of difficulties indicate some common weaknesses. Addressing spelling difficulties could include:

- ensuring letter learning is secure for all children and picking up confusions immediately they are observed; focusing on activities which match letter names with their sounds, e.g. the letter 'b' makes the sound 'b' as in book;
- ensuring children know *where* the letters to be focused on appear in words, e.g. by highlighting letters in different words at the beginning, middle and end;
- using a phonic programme based on fun approaches;
- not teaching too many similar letters at the same time;
- focusing on the differences and similarities of letters taught, and talking about them;
- teaching children that some words do not follow phonic patterns and have to be learned, e.g. high frequency words;
- using a spelling programme such as Thrass (see p60), which focuses on teaching the range of graphemes for each phoneme from the beginning, and helping children to make the correct grapheme choices;
- games to develop visual memory, e.g. Kim's game;
- teaching children the 'look, say, cover, write, check' strategy for learning spellings visually; and
- linking spellings with handwriting.

## Handwriting difficulties

These may stem from a variety of sources, including physical difficulty (fine motor problems); dyspraxia (see later section); poor formation of letters; problems with space and line; or mixing of upper and lower case letters.

*Solutions*

Strategies to address handwriting difficulties may include the following:

- the use of Information and Communication Technology (ICT) (e.g. a laptop) to relieve physical difficulty;
- careful observation of letter formation and use of multi-sensory resources (e.g. rollerball);
- teaching children to place a 'finger-space' between words;
- teaching children what a letter is and what a word is;
- attention to ascenders and descenders;
- drawing lines around whole words to 'feel' their shape;

- ensuring children know the difference between, and the purpose of, upper and lower case letters, and that both forms ('a' and 'A') match the same phoneme; and
- teaching children how to proof-read written work.

### Poor sentence structure

Examples of poor sentence structure may be words missed out; words in the wrong order; the same words repeated (e.g. in the the house); incorrect grammar (e.g. wrong verb tenses); or incorrect or non-existent punctuation.

*Solutions*

Part of the solution is to decide if errors arise from poor language skills, the writer's dialectical variations, or the writing not being edited or proof-read properly. The following strategies have been found to be helpful:

- the writer reading aloud his own work;
- response partner work, e.g. pairs of pupils identifying each other's mistakes;
- drawing attention to punctuation in shared/guided reading;
- oral games and activities to reinforce grammar;
- cloze activities, which focus on pupils inserting missing words or phrases to make the incomplete text whole; and
- modelling of standard English sentence construction by the teacher through shared and guided reading as well as through instructional writing sessions.



### Negative attitude to writing

A negative attitude to writing may arise from the lack of a positive role model for writing in the home; the fear of failure; or simply not wanting to write.

*Solutions*

It is important to establish confidence and an expectation of success. The following strategies will encourage motivation for less able writers:

- ensure writing tasks are within pupil's capabilities;
- ensure pupils know the expected writing outcome;
- provide support materials where necessary to aid writing independence, e.g. word books for high frequency words, subject dictionaries etc;
- recognise that not all pupils can produce a piece of extended writing, and put quality before quantity;
- praise even the smallest measure of success, but make sure pupils know exactly what the praise is for so that they will repeat what they have done;
- be consistent with the standards required and insist upon each child's personal best when the purpose demands it;
- recognise each child's limitations and expect only what is realistic; and
- allow time for writing to be completed to the satisfaction of the writer.

### Moving pupils on as writers

Most writing produced by the majority of pupils will benefit from improvements: moving children forward means looking at common problems and addressing them through normal lesson planning. All children benefit from regular and systematic analysis of the strengths and weaknesses of the writing being produced by the class or the year group. Questions to consider could include:

- what can writers do? What do they know about writing?
- which skills do each ability group need to develop?

- what opportunities for pupils are offered by the medium-term's writing plans? How well do they match all needs?

The following problems are to be found in most classrooms, and the strategies suggested have been found useful by the author in leading forward the following groups of writers.

*Pupils who write short sentences*

For these pupils, the following have been found to be useful:
- model extended sentences during shared/guided writing;
- practice joining sentences together as a class or group;
- have pupils underline multi-clause sentences on copied pages of text;
- talk about how longer sentences are composed, and why;
- practice activities which teach connectives; or
- write a variety of phrases on cards which can be made up into different sentence combinations for groups of pupils to work on. Research has shown that interactive group discussion is a powerful developmental factor.

*Pupils who write too much dialogue*

Children who include too much dialogue tend to get carried away with who said what, and soon lose track of the plot. The dialogue represents a ping-pong of speech, and the story goes nowhere. Strategies found useful for this include:
- focusing on the differences between prose and playscript and talking about why dialogue is sprinkled into stories;
- having pupils underline the speech and the narrative in different colours to identify the proportions of each and talk about their respective roles in a story;
- drawing attention to the way dialogue and prose are interspersed in stories, during shared/guided reading.

*Pupils unable to structure large pieces of writing*

Many pupils tend to write on, enjoying writing, but get carried away and lose sight of the story's structure, so the writing fails to hang together. These learners need to control their writing. Strategies to help this include:
- pupils planning writing in pairs, each writing part of a story, then redrafting together according to their joint plan;
- showing pupils different ways of planning writing, e.g. ideas webs, matrices, lists, network diagrams and signposting systems, as illustrated in Figures 2.4, 2.5 and 2.6.

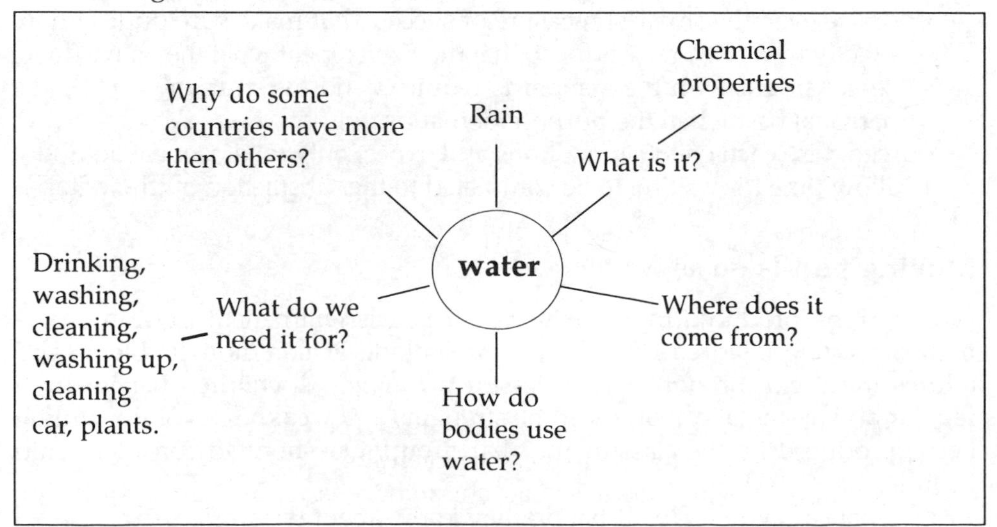


**Figure 2.4** Ideas web on the themes of water

**How and why do we use transport?**

| **Form of transport** | **Around town** | **Coming to school** | **Leisure** | **Business** |
|---|---|---|---|---|
| Bicycle | ✓ | ✓ | ✓ | ✓ |
| Bus | ✓ | ✓ | ✓ | ✓ |
| Car | ✓ | ✓ | ✓ | ✓ |
| Coach | | | ✓ | |
| Ferry | | | ✓ | ✓ |
| Helicopter | | | ✓ | ✓ |
| Lorry | ✓ | | | ✓ |
| Motorbike | ✓ | | ✓ | |
| Plane | | | ✓ | ✓ |
| Ship | | | | |
| Train | ✓ | | ✓ | ✓ |
| Van | ✓ | | ✓ | ✓ |

**Figure 2.5** Matrix on the theme of transport

| Main heading | <a> Healthy eating |
|---|---|
| <b> as subset of <a> | <b> Vitamins and minerals |
| <c> as subsets of <b> | <c> What are they? |
| | <c> Why do we need them? |
| | <c> Which foods contain them? |

**Figure 2.6** Structuring headings – theme 'Healthy eating'

*Pupils reluctant to redraft*

Many children enjoy writing but, having written the first draft, cannot be bothered to revise it. Encourage them by:

- ensuring that redrafting is done only when necessary;
- ensuring a good first draft so that redrafting is not too laborious;
- varying the drafting strategies, e.g. individual, as pairs, as groups, using cut and paste, or underlining parts which could be improved; or
- providing a real audience and making clear when the redrafting is part of the writing process.

*Pupils who fail to focus on a larger piece of writing*

Many children find it hard to concentrate on extended writing although their writing skills are adequate. They simply get 'fed up', so helping them to focus on the task may be a main objective. Strategies for support include:

- using a kitchen timer when writing, increasing the task time gradually as pupils progress;
- ensuring pupils know why you are training their concentration and how they will benefit;
- making writing tasks as real and as purposeful as possible;
- splitting writing tasks with other activities in between;
- varying writing activities to increase interest;
- providing positive feedback as children achieve improved spans of concentration;

- providing gentle, soothing music as a background to the writing task; and
- sometimes offering pupils choice to ensure relevance and help sustain interest.

## Writing and SEN

Focused instruction set against an atmosphere of high expectations should reduce writing difficulties, but the principle of high expectation needs to be balanced against small steps of progression. For the least able, some NLS objectives will have to be broken down into finely graded targets, and success for children with SEN depends on how effectively the NLS links with the Code of Practice. Systems need to be manageable, yet enable writing progress for all.

### The SEN Code of Practice

The Code of Practice for the Identification and Assessment of Special Educational Needs (DfE 1994) identifies five stages of educational provision.

Children at **Stage 1** of the Code are those whose progress has given cause for concern: placing children at Stage 1 identifies the need for differentiated teaching to address difficulties, and access to NLS teaching should enable the majority of children at Stage 1 to keep up.

Children who do not make sufficient progress through access alone may move to **Stage 2** of the Code, following a review. These children have an IEP, which identifies their learning difficulties and the action taken to address them. Provision at Stage 2 is the responsibility of the school. Access to the NLS, together with some additional support, may enable some of these children to revert to Stage 1, or be removed from the SEN register altogether.

Children who make very little progress at Stage 2, following an IEP review, may be moved to **Stage 3** of the Code and may receive additional intervention from external SEN specialists. This, much smaller, group of children will have acute learning difficulties. Their IEPs will be based upon careful assessment over a period of time, reflected by the targets identified.

A small proportion of children who still do not make progress may be referred to the Local Education Authority (LEA) for formal assessment (**Stage 4**) which may, or may not, result in a statement of SEN at **Stage 5** of the Code. Children with statements for SEN usually receive additional resources from the LEA; Chapter 10 expands on how additional resources may be best used to enable writing progress.

You may be questioning what the Code of Practice has to do with writing for all. The success of the NLS depends upon maximum numbers of children with SEN making significantly better progress in literacy. This is more likely to happen if IEPs are linked with NLS objectives and additional human resources effectively support both.

### IEPs

If the NLS is effective, numbers on SEN registers should decline, resulting in fewer IEPs and less SENCO time spent writing literacy targets. But, for some children, breaking NLS objectives into small progressive steps may be a constant and necessary part of their educational entitlement. All pupils with SEN can and should be involved in their learning targets and should be encouraged to accept some degree of ownership.

#### *IEP targets*

Targets on IEPs should identify what a pupil will do, know or understand by the end of a stated time-scale. Strategies identify what the schools or external agencies will do to enable pupils to achieve them. SMART targets are:

- simple — for everyone (including the child) to understand;
- measurable — for achievement to be assessed;
- achievable — match what pupils can realistically do;
- relevant — to the pupil's goals and interests; and
- timed — to promote a rigorous approach towards progress.

## Targets for writing

A return to the case studies mentioned earlier may now be useful in the light of the above points. Writing targets for Anna may be agreed as:

- to spell 50 words from NLS List 1, Years 1 to 2;
- to use upper and lower case letters correctly.

The question is how many spellings children with similar difficulties to Anna can realistically learn within the term of an IEP. Too high a target will invite failure, and too low a target will defeat the NLS principles of high expectations and pace. Writing targets for Alan could be:

- to write two sentences unaided;
- to produce neat handwriting.

The need is to eliminate anxiety and prevent failure. Alan has been taught cursive writing too soon; letters are wrongly formed and the problem is now acute. ICT could be part of the rescue strategy for Alan, and children with similar problems.

Darren's targets may need to start small, and gradually build up. Targets could be:

- to spell 10 words from NLS List 1;
- to write (his) own caption for a picture.

For many children with similar problems to Darren, writing unaided becomes a main objective if they have been dependent on adults for spellings. Their confidence must be restored, to enable skills to be taught and practised. Children with writing problems other than handwriting often disguise them with remarkable success.

## Linking NLS objectives with pupil targets

The majority of NLS objectives for writing composition allow pupils to access the objective at a level appropriate to their learning. Pupils with the difficulties explored above could therefore access the following objectives, and achieve them at their own level:

*Year 1, Term 2:*

- to write labels for drawings and diagrams;
- to write simple questions.

*Year 2, Term 3:*

- to make simple notes from non-fiction texts;
- to write non-chronological reports . . .

*Year 5, Term 1:*

- to record ideas, reflections and predictions . . .;
- to write instructional texts and test them out . . .

Children with SEN can achieve in writing composition without necessarily improving their spelling or handwriting.

Many NLS objectives for word and sentence work recognise the need for continued reinforcement. Consider these objectives:

- to secure reading and spelling of all the high frequency words in Appendix List 1 (Year 2, Term 3);
- to practise new spellings regularly by 'look, say, cover, write, check' strategy (Year 3, Term 1);
- to revise and extend work on verbs (Year 5, Term 1).

Careful integration of IEP targets with NLS objectives will support manageability from both perspectives.

## Areas of SEN which affect writing progress

Two forms of SEN have a potentially debilitating affect upon writing progress: dyspraxia, which affects mainly handwriting, and dyslexia, which affects mainly spelling.

### *Dyspraxia*

Dyspraxia is a term used to describe a developmental coordination disorder. Addy (1998) writes that, 'this lack of coordination has repercussions on the child's handwriting legibility, (and) organisation in the classroom'. Research has shown that 5.3 per cent of the population suffer from a lack of coordination and do not achieve their academic potential. Addy suggests that children with dyspraxia will benefit from focused work on:

- visual memory, e.g. re-piecing cut up pictures;
- hand-eye coordination, e.g. tracking activities;
- visual sequential memory, e.g. remembering lists of things;
- figure ground discrimination, e.g. finding hidden objects; and
- visual closure, e.g. envisaging wrapped presents, or completing parts of pictures and well known shapes.

Helping children with dyspraxia to develop their handwriting means using a multi-sensory approach, for example, tracing letters in sand, and using tactile aids wherever possible. Specialist advice for a child with suspected dyspraxia is essential.

### *Dyslexia*

Dyslexia is more often referred to as a specific learning difficulty (SpLD), and is one of eight categories of SEN with a separate section in the SEN Code of Practice 1994.

Smith (1996) suggests that people with SpLD have problems with:

- *synthesising* — bringing together information in the brain;
- *organising* — making sense of this information; and
- *memorising* — holding on to information to use at will.

Spelling is the overwhelming problem for all dyslexics. The problem with trying to identify children with dyslexia at an early age is that many children have developmental spelling problems, but few children with spelling difficulties emerge as genuinely dyslexic. Once diagnosed, dyslexia is not easily dealt with.

Smith (1996) lists some performance indicators which may suggest the need for focused assessment by a specialist:

- poor literacy is inconsistent with adequate work in other curriculum areas;
- performance varies from day to day;
- oral language is usually at a higher level than written;
- reading lacks fluency;

- taught core words are not retained;
- spelling is bizarre and uncommunicable;
- multi-syllabic words may be mispronounced; or
- sequencing skills are a problem, e.g. remembering days of the week, the next lesson, when to bring PE kit.

It is essential to identify dyslexia as early as possible and to seek specialist advice and support. Chapter 7 expands on how best to support dyslexic learners with their spelling.

This chapter has explored writing problems in the context of the NLS and the Code of Practice. Further issues associated with spelling, handwriting and composition are explored in later chapters.

*Chapter 3*

# Becoming a Writer

How do learners become effective and communicative writers? All children need to see themselves as writers from the beginning. Their own perceptions, at the scribble stage during role play, are a start to the process leading to their development as competent writers. All educators need to understand the process in order to help struggling learners.

## *Developing writing*

Writing is such a complex activity that it is often difficult to separate the skills involved in order to identify and address pupils' writing difficulties. It may be helpful to look at writing skills in two strands, as illustrated in Figure 3.1.

| Skills — writing conventions | Strategies — shape/form |
|---|---|
| letter formation | identifying purpose |
| spellings | identifying audience |
| sentence structure | deciding on format |
| use of grammar | organisation |
| punctuation | using writing to learn |
| text structure (paragraphs, chapters) | using visual form (e.g. matrix or chart) |
| cursive handwriting | |

**Figure 3.1** Strands of writing growth

The conventions of writing could be thought of as the skills and knowledge writers need to develop at word, sentence and text level, which emerge as secretarial skills, e.g. forming letters, punctuation and spelling. The writer is not the initiator of those skills, but knows they are to be learned, and that writing will not progress well without them.

Giving writing a recognised shape and form according to the criteria listed in Figure 3.1 offers the developing writer some control over the process. If the purpose is his own, the writer has to think about how best to present his work for his chosen readers: these thought elements could be seen as writing strategies to adapt writing for the proposed readership.

Each strand of growth can develop at a different rate, leaving the other behind. A young person can reach Key Stage 4 or beyond, having learned to spell, produce perfect handwriting and well constructed paragraphs, yet be unable to vary their writing style: a letter to a friend will be written in the same style as one applying for a job. Conversely, a learner may have a range of writing styles, be able to write in different forms, yet have almost illegible handwriting and/or poor spelling. To achieve balance, both strands of growth should mark the development of writing, as different skills and strategies, from the pre-writer to National Curriculum Level 4 and beyond.

Much has been written about the emergent writing approach, which uses a child's readiness to write and his own developmental pace as instructional guidelines. The emergent writing principle deviates from the NLS principle of teaching writing to all children as part of a carefully structured sequence following a pre-determined pace. Rather like the Pied Piper, the NLS calls the tune and expects all children to follow and keep up.

For children with learning difficulties, a balanced approach recognises the fine line between tugging children's writing forward to suit the pace of teaching, and inviting frustration and failure for some learners. One key issue is how and when to speed up the emergent process at a pace which matches the NLS Framework objectives, yet enables effective learning.

### Attitudes and expectations

A pupil's attitude to writing is as important as his learned skills and strategies. How learners think about writing influences the effort they put in and the time they freely devote to developing their skills. The National Writing Project (1989) questioned teachers on their expectations of the developing writer. They expected children to be:

- risk-takers – willing to experiment with new forms and functions;
- collaborators – able to develop writing through negotiation and collaboration with others;
- responders – developing a critical response to own writing and that of others; and
- confident writers – knowing own strengths and limitations.

Attempts to match age groups with these expectations are fraught with problems. Attitudes to writing such as those listed above need to develop as early as possible in a child's life, and become more sophisticated as writing develops. Children should also be able to see writing as an enjoyable activity – after all, many people choose to spend their working lives writing. Inviting authors of different genres into school can help learners to see the other side of writing. The locality is full of writers, many of whom offer their services to stimulate children's interest in writing. Try approaching local Arts Councils or writers' groups. You may discover people who write novels set in the local region; write poems (and possibly have long hair and earrings); write a regular column in the weekly newspaper; interview unusual characters and do write-ups about them; write articles for magazines; write stories for children; or write plays.

Enabling children who experience initial difficulties to persevere and not become disillusioned is difficult, relying on a thorough awareness by teachers of how 'mark-makers' eventually emerge as writers.

#### *Children's views of writing*

The way in which children view writing will influence their progress, and almost certainly reflects the models of writing they observe at school and at home. Consider the comments in Figure 3.2 from children about writing.It is easy to spot the comments from struggling writers as opposed to competent ones.

## *Becoming a writer – the stages*

Writing is a process which takes years to complete. Many learners never complete it. At the first hurdle some stop and become persistent refusers, others complete the course but trail in among the last, and even among the winners are those for whom the end prize holds little value.

### Writing in the early stages

Gorman and Brooks (1996) identified seven stages of early writing development, the first five of which occur before children even reach National

Curriculum Level 1. These early stages are mainly working towards National Curriculum Level 1 in writing.

| | |
|---|---|
| Writing is putting words in sentences. | Why do we have to write in all lessons? |
| Writing helps you get a job and make money. | I hate writing. Dad says we shouldn't have homework. |
| Writing is a bit like thinking . . . it helps you organise things. | Poetry is stupid. People with long hair and earrings write poetry. It doesn't make sense. |
| My teacher says she can't read my writing. | I wish we could take our time. Copying makes my hand hurt. |
| I'm afraid to write because it won't come out right. All my words get mixed up. | My spellings are all wrong. I'll never get them right. |
| If we could write onto the computer my handwriting wouldn't matter. | There's too much to think about . . . my teacher goes on about spellings . . . and I keep missing words out . . . |

**Figure 3.2** Comments from children about writing

The first stage is that of drawing and sign writing. Scribbles and shapes bear little resemblance to letters, but the writer knows the difference between pictures and words.

Through stages 2, 3 and 4, young children are gradually learning to form the shapes of individual letters, and writing starts to resemble English script. There may or may not be spaces in between groups of letters. At these stages writing takes place by children writing over, then under the teacher's writing. Copying writing gradually results in children writing many letters correctly without help.

Gorman and Brooks (1996) describe Stage 4 as the 'taking-off point when children learn the fundamental idea of how to communicate meaning in writing'. At Stage 5, children have 'crossed the threshold to literacy', and are associating the sounds of groups of letters with spoken words. From this point, children can express concepts through their writing.

A key issue for the nursery or reception teacher is when and how to seize on writing readiness in order to spontaneously guide it forward. Many believe that the time to start writing is when words are already familiar friends. Once a child can read a few words, e.g. his own name, family names, toys, words on cereal packets, school words and so on, it seems natural to want to make those words himself. The starting point must be with words a child wants to write, and which hold significance and relevance in his world. First steps in writing must not appear to the learner as a strange and irrelevant experience.

## Writing at Key Stage 1

The average child should leave Key Stage 1 having achieved National Curriculum Level 2 in writing. Two questions emerge: how do learners progress towards National Curriculum Level 2 from the early stages of writing? And how are these developmental writing skills represented in the National Curriculum and the NLS?

It is helpful to reflect that NLS objectives represent what is to be taught, while National Curriculum levels describe what ought to have been learned. As the examples illustrate, there is a recognised time lapse between the teaching and learning of writing skills and strategies. Consider some requirements of National Curriculum Levels 1 and 2:

National Curriculum Level 1 writing:

- communicates meaning — through simple words and phrases;
- shows awareness of full stops;
- has letters clearly shaped, and correctly oriented.

National Curriculum Level 2 writing:

- uses narrative and non-narrative forms;
- uses appropriate and interesting vocabulary;
- shows some awareness of the reader;
- sequences sentences, with some capitals and full stops;
- has monosyllabic words spelt correctly, and alternatives phonetically plausible;
- has letters accurately formed, and consistent in size.

### *What do we look for?*

At Level 1, writing shows clear communication of a message. The writer may, for example, indicate in writing what he liked or disliked about a particular book. Events are written in a straightforward sequence. In order to write simple words, there must be some use of phonic strategies, along with a developing graphic knowledge and some spelling of known words, e.g. high-frequency words from NLS List 1. Letters should have clear ascenders and descenders. The need for a mere 'awareness' of full stops implies inconsistent use by the Level 1 writer.

The Level 2 writer communicates meaning beyond a simple statement, and is able to write in a range of forms, meeting the needs of his audience to some degree. There is some coherence and some control over syntax. Handwriting is clear, though not necessarily joined. There is evidence of spelling skills and strategies being applied, e.g. where words are incorrect they are phonetically plausible.

### *NLS objectives – Year 1 and 2*

The NLS objectives illustrate a clear relationship with the National Curriculum, based upon the time lapse between what is taught and what is learned. Consider the following Key Stage 1 sample objectives from the NLS Framework:

*Year 1 – word level work:*

- to represent in writing . . . three phonemes in CVC words;
- spell common irregular words from Appendix List 1;
- to segment words into phonemes for spelling;
- to form lower case letters correctly;
- to learn spellings of verbs with '-ed' and '-ing' endings;
- to make collections of personal interest or. significant words.

*Year 1 – sentence level work:*

- to continue . . . ending a sentence with a full stop;
- to add question marks to questions.

*Year 1 – text level work:*

- to write about events (and) familiar incidents from stories;
- make simple lists for planning and reminding;
- to compose own poetic sentences;
- to use the language and features of non-fiction texts;
- to write own questions.

## *Analysis*

From the NLS sample objectives, preparation for achievement at National Curriculum Level 2 is apparent. For example, the teaching of narrative and non-narrative forms of writing is a constant feature throughout the NLS objectives, even at this stage. Children are 'collecting' vocabulary and adding to their repertoire of known words ready to 'use appropriate and interesting vocabulary' at National Curriculum Level 2. Pupils are 'taught to form lower case letters correctly', and there is reference to phonic and graphic spelling to match the National Curriculum Level 2 requirement to spell monosyllabic words.

Now consider writing at National Curriculum Levels 3 and 4. At National Curriculum Level 3:

- writing is organised, imaginative and clear;
- use of different writing forms . . . adapted to readers;
- words are chosen for variety and interest;
- sentence structure is usually correct;
- spelling is accurate — including polysyllabic words;
- evidence of full stops, capitals, question marks;
- handwriting is joined and legible.

At National Curriculum Level 4:

- writing in a range of forms is lively and thoughtful;
- ideas are sustained;
- writing is organised for the purpose and the reader;
- vocabulary is adventurous — used for effect;
- writer uses grammatically complex sentences;
- spelling is generally accurate;
- punctuation is used within the sentence (e.g. commas);
- handwriting is fluent, joined and legible.

Now consider the following NLS objectives from Year 2. Note that many from Year 1 are revisited.

*Year 2 - word level work:*

- to secure . . . spelling of long vowel digraphs;
- to revise and extend the . . . spelling of . . . long vowel phonemes from Year 1.

*Year 2 - sentence level work:*

- other uses of capitalisation;
- find examples of . . . words and phrases that link sentences.

*Year 2 - text level work:*

- to produce simple flow charts or diagrams;
- write sustained stories;
- make simple notes from non-fiction texts.

## *Analysis*

The NLS samples illustrate Year 2 preparation for National Curriculum Level 3, with some reference to National Curriculum Level 4. For example, there is NLS reference to 'sustained stories', reflecting the 'sustained ideas' from National Curriculum Level 4. The National Curriculum requirement to use grammatically complex sentences echoes the Year 2 NLS reference to 'words and phrases that link sentences'.

The National Curriculum Level 4 requirement to 'write in a range of forms' echoes the NLS Year 2 reference to producing flow charts and diagrams and making notes from non-fiction texts. Clearly, NLS teaching objectives from Year 2 are a start to preparing pupils for achievement at National Curriculum Level 3 and beyond.

### Writing at Key Stage 2

Many NLS objectives for Key Stage 2 continue from those already introduced. From Year 3, word level work contains much revision and consolidation. There is a noticeable shift to spelling strategies, conventions and rules, as well as vocabulary extension, with a clear indication that pupils are to consolidate acquired skills, and develop effective strategies for using them throughout Key Stage 2.

By the end of Year 4, consistent practise to develop fluency and speed in handwriting should have resulted in, 'joined handwriting for all writing except where special forms are required'. During Key Stage 2, sentence and text level work build on from Key Stage 1, with an emphasis on strategies for using and extending writing skills already taught.

### Summary of National Curriculum progression

*Consistency in Teacher Assessment – Exemplification of Standards* was produced by the School Curriculum and Assessment Authority (SCAA) in 1995. The booklet contains samples of cross-curricular writing with clear explanations for each judgement. The National Curriculum recognises that children's writing develops in different contexts over time, and the Level descriptions identify significant features of writing at particular levels. A summary of the broad lines of progression is useful at this point.

From Level 1 it is important for children to start to control the mechanical processes and the conventions of written language. The understanding of sound/symbol relationships and letter strings at Level 1 forms the basis for spelling increasingly complex words.

From Level 2, children's growing understanding of how texts are organised differently should be seen through varied vocabulary, sentence construction and shaping of writing for a range of purposes. There should be a greater competence and flexibility, demonstrated from writing across the curriculum.

At Levels 3 and 4, children should be confident in extending their range of writing. From this, learner writers continue to control, refine and adapt their styles to suit their purpose and audience.

#### *Adaptation for meaning and effect*

SCAA (1995) reminds schools that the impact of writing and its interest to the reader are significant at each National Curriculum level as well as an ongoing theme of overall assessment. Children's growing ability to use their skills as strategies in adapting their writing to suit the shape and form of work required reflect the degree of challenge in the task, its purpose and its audience.

## *Becoming a writer – SEN implications*

For children with SEN, their handicap will start in Key Stage 1, the moment they fail to grasp the writing skills which need to be built on during Key Stage 2. As difficulties are first noticed, catch-up intervention must be implemented so that the key skills of spelling, handwriting and sentence or text construction are secured for as many pupils as possible before they leave Key Stage 1.

Emphasis on the skills and conventions of writing should not neglect the development of shape and form. This is one reason why children with writing difficulties need to reinforce their skills through different learning contexts so that writing does not become stale, and learners do not become demotivated.

### Becoming a speller

The child who spells well is not one who has learned the rules of spelling, but the child who reads a great deal. Reading encourages children to visualise the words they need, and helps them to see if words they have spelled 'look right'. The way children see words as they read plays a large part in their attempts to spell them. Learners who read mainly by the whole word method may have difficulty with segmenting words into their constituent phonemes, then selecting graphemes. Conversely, children who have been taught to read alphabetically spell badly because they are hearing words rather than visualising them. The result may be something like, 'On Wensdy we ave a spelin lesn'.

Children need to use both strategies. When learning to spell high-frequency words from NLS lists, learners must be aware that these words have to be visually learned, but on the other hand, they must have the phonic strategies with which to attempt new words in order to become independent spellers.

### *Stages of spelling knowledge*

Gentry (1987), among others, has demonstrated that for all learners, spelling follows a sequential process. At the pre-communicative stage, children express meaning through random letters, as illustrated in Figure 3.3; at the semi-phonetic stage, learners are attempting to match sounds with their corresponding letters, but many are still missed out, especially vowels; at the phonetic stage, learners are making systematic efforts to match sounds with letters and letter clusters, as illustrated in Figure 3.4; at the transitional stage, reliance on phonic strategies starts to shift towards a greater reliance on visual strategies, as learners make analogies from words they can already spell; and finally, by the correct stage, children have a good knowledge of how words are constructed in order to make correct choices, and have an extensive repertoire of known words.

I had a bath.

**Figure 3.3** Sample of pre-communicative writing

Krikit.
it waw a ferar game that day of
krikit I lost and Egun wun
the skiy was bluy with wite
clads in. The boll went hey
sutims.

**Figure 3.4** Sample of phonetic spelling

Most children are expected to reach the phonetic stage by the end of Key Stage 1, having attained National Curriculum Level 2, with spellings that are 'phonetically plausible'.

Half-way through Key Stage 2, at approximately National Curriculum Level 3, spellings are well through the transitional stage, i.e. 'usually accurate'. By National Curriculum Level 4, at the correct stage, all spellings are generally accurate. By this stage, children are able to see when a word does not look right, and identify what is wrong with it, as visual strategies have taken over from phonetic ones. The correct speller has enough known words from which to make analogies when spelling new words.

*Enhancing spelling development for children with SEN*

1. Develop writing from the mark-making stage by:
   - presenting children with varied writing materials;
   - stimulation, i.e. through shared and guided writing;
   - involving the child in a variety of writing tasks; and
   - accepting what is offered and giving plenty of feedback.

2. As marks start to become letter-like shapes, lead writing forward by:
   - asking the child to read out his communication;
   - linking his type of message to others in the classroom as models and talking about them;
   - talking about letters and words; and
   - talking about letter names and sounds and linking these with the letter shapes being taught.

3. As children start to include more known letters in their writing and demonstrate their knowledge of letters for sounds, move them along by:
   - consolidating previous learning;
   - alphabet games and letter formation activities;
   - asking children to read out their writing;
   - linking specific letter-like shapes with their known names and sounds;
   - extending phonic knowledge through shared reading and writing;
   - talking about words;
   - continuing to focus on rhythm and rhyme in words.
   - developing the range of strategies used to spell, e.g. the use of word lists and dictionaries;
   - stressing the 'look, cover, say, write, check' method to develop learners' visual strategies for spelling;
   - providing word search activities which focus on seeing whole words from a mass of print; and
   - developing pupils' perceptions of themselves as 'good spellers'.

4. As children realise that not all words look like they sound, help them along by all of the above strategies. In addition:
   - promote interest in word investigation and patterns;
   - look at structures and common word endings, e.g. -ed, -ing;
   - teach children how to proof-read by focusing on how words 'look', and using their graphic knowledge;
   - have children locate and correct deliberate mistakes; and
   - use response partners to proof-read each other's writing.

5. Finally, the learner has reached the point where spelling is largely correct. He may think that, 'words are difficult. There are all these rules to remember.' This progress towards correct spelling is encouraged by:
   - emphasising the high proportions of words and parts which are correct;
   - insisting that children identify their own errors;
   - using spell checkers to rectify minor errors;
   - relate vocabulary development to the principles of spelling where appropriate; and

- have children explore meanings of words, and their derivations in groups.

*Pupils with acute spelling difficulties*

For any child with an acute spelling problem, for example, a child with dyslexia, an established long-term strategy could operate from the following principles:

- if spelling is a main priority, do not allow other areas of learning to overshadow it;
- know the words to be learned and stick to them;
- make targets realistic for the learner;
- allow learners to choose words from identified lists;
- name an assigned helper for 'catch-up' work;
- involve parents in the joint effort; and
- remember that 'little and often' works best.

There is a lot to be said for pupils being allowed to choose their own spellings to be learned, as motivation is greatly enhanced by doing this. The 'my own words' example illustrated in Figure 3.5 is based on words the pupil has spelt incorrectly, while ensuring the words picked up are those from among the priority lists.

| **My own words** | | | |
|---|---|---|---|
| **Name** Emma | **Year** 4R | **Week beginning** Feb 4th | |
| **Common words** | | **Subject words** | |
| wrong ✗ | right ✓ | wrong ✗ | right ✓ |
| thay | they | culor | colour |
| wen | when | sed | said |

**Figure 3.5** Learning to spell from 'my own words'

The child with poor spelling will also benefit from linking spelling with handwriting. It is generally agreed that a joined hand promotes improved spelling, as children get the 'feel' of words.

## Developing handwriting

Asking children to write formal letters too soon could result in bad habits which are difficult to cure. A programme which develops motor control as a basis for good writing patterns is worth embarking on before the start of formal handwriting instruction. Activities could include:

- forming patterns in different media – clay, sand, plasticine;
- writing in thick crayons and pencils;
- making patterns which follow a particular direction – left to right, top to bottom, clockwise and anti-clockwise, and diagonal.

*Pupils with handwriting difficulties*

The child with a recognised, long-standing problem with handwriting will benefit from:

- a whole-school consistent policy from the letter formation to the cursive stage;
- handwriting practice that is linked with spelling;
- handwriting practice based on words the child can read;

- not too much at once; and
- the use of a laptop for presentation of writing where necessary.

It is also essential to focus on the main priority when developing handwriting. A child with severe motor control problems cannot concentrate and develop several areas of handwriting at once. Is the main handwriting target to form letters correctly, to produce letters of consistent size in relation to line, to space out words, to produce neatly printed letters, or to join letters? It is best to choose one main priority and to work first on achieving this.

This chapter has explored the development of writing using the NLS as the teaching context, with the National Curriculum as staging points at which learning is assessed.

While writing remains an integrated experience, teaching must take account of its constituent parts – handwriting, spelling and composition – in order to guide learners forward. In order for children with learning difficulties to become writers, catch-up strategies need to focus clearly on problem areas as they arise. A policy for writing will have at its heart the need for all learners to achieve a balanced progression through each strand of growth.

*Chapter 4*

# Writing – Policy and Planning

A policy of 'writing for all' reflects the NLS Framework for teaching as a national long-term plan for raising literacy standards. The policy may start with a statement of the philosophy and principles underpinning writing for all in the school, and may also include a section for each of the sub-skills summarised in Figure 4.1.

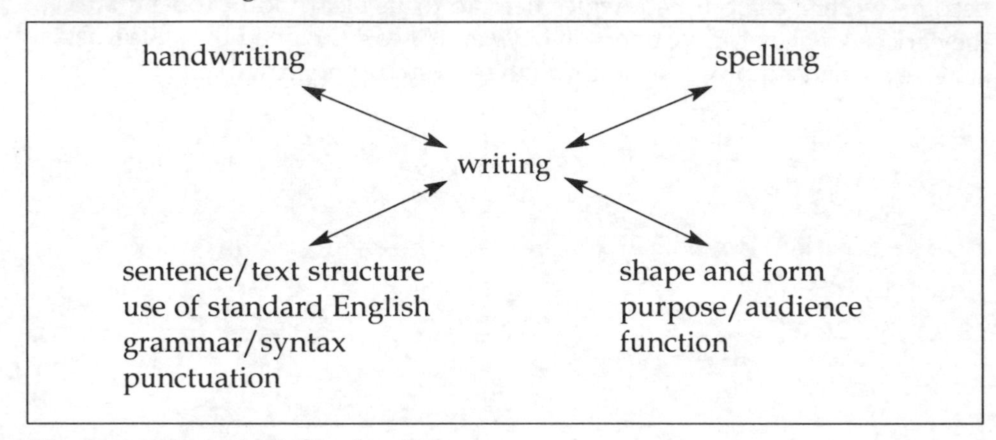


**Figure 4.1** The sub-skills of writing

## Philosophy

The NLS Framework implies a philosophy of:

- high expectations – all children can become writers, given the right learning environment;
- entitlement – the literacy hour is for all children;
- inclusion – all children learn better alongside peers;
- positive attitudes – of teachers and pupils towards writing (and reading); and
- modelling and guiding writing – working with the whole class and in groups.

School philosophy about writing needs to reflect the views and beliefs held by the team of professionals who share in its teaching; after all, they deliver policy through their practice. School staff are likely to have quite different ideas on how writing should be taught, and what constitutes a good writer. Staff may feel a good writer should do some or all of the following:

- interest a range of readers;
- write accurately, e.g. use correct spelling, punctuation and sentence structure;
- work independently and be able to use support materials;
- write in a range of styles and a variety of formats; and
- show commitment and perseverance in redrafting work.

Different staff are likely to place importance on different qualities.

### *The teacher's role*

Part of the philosophy may be based on how teachers see their roles with regard to developing pupils' writing. Staff may see themselves as sources of ideas; collectors of resources; readers; assessors of pupils' writing; or as editors and proof-readers.

In the context of the NLS, teachers are also perceived as:

- modellers – during shared writing;
- guides – during guided writing;
- facilitators – providing opportunities based on needs; and
- managers and organisers – of integrated writing activities in and out of the literacy hour.

The fresh role of teachers in literacy development as schools move towards the millennium is an important philosophical consideration.

### *Developmental or traditional?*

How should writing be taught? This question stirs up many conflicting views on writing methodology. Is writing best taught traditionally, or learned developmentally? Both approaches could have advantages and disadvantages as listed in Figure 4.2.

| **Writing learned developmentally** | **Writing taught traditionally** |
|---|---|
| involves thinking | involves a lot of copying |
| writer takes risks | writer afraid to be wrong |
| writer can experiment | writer usually conforms |
| writing rarely corrected | writing often over-corrected |
| writer chooses own purpose | teacher is main purpose |
| system is learned gradually | writing system is presented |
| writing is for the reader | writing is for assessment |
| writing is shared | writing is solitary |
| writer tries spellings | writer is given spellings |
| writer develops independence | writer depends on others |

**Figure 4.2** Traditional or developmental writing approach?

The issue of which approach is best for children with SEN would receive different responses from teachers, based on their own experiences of teaching writing: the writer who is never corrected will take longer to address his problems; less able writers who have been victims of the 'red pen' too often lose the heart to keep trying; and the developmental writer has the confidence to write unaided, seeing process as opposed to 'wrongness' or 'rightness'. On the other hand, spelling has to be taught alongside the process of writing: children who are given spellings are less likely to try for themselves.

The NLS philosophy of writing combines traditional and developmental approaches, based on vigorous instruction, with opportunities to reinforce what is taught in other contexts. A policy for writing recognises that all children learn more effectively by sharing writing, talking about it, seeing good writing models and receiving constructive criticism and guidance towards writing goals. Many traditional methods sit quite comfortably within an atmosphere of experimentation and risk-taking. The above points are intended as a starting point to whole-school discussions on staff attitudes and beliefs about writing, which help to shape policy.

## Principles of the writing policy

Where staff share, or agree to compromise on, principles, the teaching of writing is more likely to be consistent across and between key stages. The following principles could form part of a school's policy for writing and influence other school policies (e.g. parental partnership).

1. *Range and reality*
All children should have opportunities to explore writing, experimenting with the range of writing formats, purposes and audiences. Many writing tasks could have a real outcome. The writing policy could list ideas for real writing activities for various classes, which could include the following:

- Stage 2 children writing stories for Key Stage 1;
- writing a booklet for visitors to their town, to be sold in the local Tourist Information Bureau;
- writing labels on cupboards in the classroom;
- writing a play to be performed by the writers or by another class or group, e.g. the Christmas play;
- older children writing simple subject dictionaries for Key Stage 1 class-rooms to aid access to subject reading; or
- children writing their own notices for the school jumble sale, craft fair etc.

Writing tasks rooted in reality will motivate less able learners to be part of the action.

2. *Writing as part of language and literacy*
It is widely recognised that all aspects of language and literacy enrich each other. A policy of writing for all recognises the relationship between reading and writing, and their dependency upon speaking and listening. In practice, language and literacy develop together: shared writing usually involves shared reading, with interactive discussion, and phonic work supports the blending of graphemes for reading, and the segmentation of phonemes for spelling.

3. *Equal opportunities*
The policy should state how groups of pupils are to access the writing curriculum. How are all children included in writing activities? What support systems operate, human or material, and how are various groups of learners with SEN helped to make the best use of writing opportunities in school?

4. *A balanced approach*
How does the policy combine positive elements of traditional and developmental writing approaches? The NLS recognises that children need to be explicitly taught, yet they require time and space to experiment and become masters of their own learning.

5. *Teaching and learning*
Does the policy recognise the difference between what is taught and what is learned? Does it state how writing skills and strategies are reinforced through other subject work?

6. *Parts and wholes*
A policy for literacy reflects a clear relationship between skills teaching and the whole context. Writing is often taught in parts, i.e. letters, words, parts of sentences, and even at text level, the emphasis may be on a specific element,

e.g. punctuation. All learners must see how the parts of writing fit into the whole context in order to become writers.

7. *Breadth and balance*
A policy of writing for all ensures that both strands of growth develop together. Spelling or handwriting difficulties should not be allowed to overshadow composition. Writing activities need to balance work on spelling, handwriting and structure with the development of shape and form.

8. *Pupil ownership*
How far does the policy promote pupil ownership of their own goals? Knowing what they are aiming for helps children, especially those with SEN, to focus on specific aspects of their writing.

9. *Parental partnership*
The NLS recognises that professionals cannot do it all. Research indicates that parental responsibility and sharing in the development of literacy skills is vital to success. What is the policy for enabling as many parents as possible to share responsibility for writing progress? How does the policy attempt to include the parents of children with SEN?

10. *Moving learners on*
Progress in writing has to start from children's current level of ability and move them on accordingly. The policy needs to balance out blocked work on writing for all learners, differentiated in its delivery (composition), with ongoing, focused attention to individual writing difficulties (e.g. spelling).

11. *Display areas*
Finally, what principles underpin the effective use of display areas, and how are they best used for the benefit of reading and writing?

Many of these principles are expanded upon in later chapters.

## Procedures

Success for all children depends on a common approach to teaching writing. Research indicates that children perform better when there is consistency between year groups and key stages. A policy for all learners should include statements on the following elements of writing.

### *Handwriting policy*

A basic handwriting policy would identify the following:

- the role of handwriting as part of the writing process;
- examples of handwriting from the early stages onwards to illustrate key points and to promote consistent responses to children's handwriting;
- the school's choice of a particular style, scheme or approach to handwriting, with a brief explanation of the reason. Is the first printing plain, or does each letter have an upward or outward 'joining flick' to support the transition to cursive writing?

The following questions may support whole-school discussion on handwriting policy:

- what pre-handwriting activities are available?
- in which order are letters taught and why?
- how much time is devoted to handwriting practice?
- what is the agreed use of lined and unlined paper?
- what is the agreed policy for supporting left-handedness?

- what about the needs of bilingual children, particularly if their first language is written from right to left?
- how is handwriting to be assessed, marked and recorded in a consistent manner?
- how is the teaching of handwriting to be managed?
- how is the practice of handwriting to be extended across the curriculum?

*Handwriting difficulties*

Some children, e.g. those with dyspraxia, have genuine problems with any activities which include writing. For some learners, handwriting may not fully progress towards a neat, cursive style. A policy for handwriting needs to identify how handwriting difficulties are to be accommodated by sensitive responses. Areas of discussion may include:

- the use of Information and Communication Technology (ICT) where possible in cases of genuine physical difficulty, and the provision of laptops where these are identified on IEPs or statements;
- the need for extra time for some children to produce the desired standards; and
- recognition of when handwriting matters and when it does not.

*Spelling policy*

NLS policy recognises the clear link between phonics for spelling and for reading, and that each supports the development of the other. In looking at school spelling policy, it may be helpful to consider the following questions:

1. What strategies are children taught to help them learn spellings? Are they taught to:
   - segment phonetically-regular words to identify their components?
   - use the 'look, cover, say, write and check' strategy to learn irregular words (e.g. from NLS lists)?
   - copy out words as an aid to spelling?
   - say the letter names as they write them?

2. What classroom time is given to spelling and children's difficulties, and how is this combined with handwriting where appropriate? Is this time in the literacy hour, out of it, or both?

3. Which spellings are to be systematically learned?
   - the NLS high-frequency words?
   - reading scheme words?
   - core vocabulary for subject writing as necessary?
   - words from each child's individual errors?
   - collated lists from the common incorrect spellings of the class, focused on at regular intervals?

4. How many spellings should be learned each day or week? For some children the target may be five words per week, while other children may manage twenty.

5. How do teachers consistently monitor progress in spelling? Is this through class testing each week of the spelling lists identified, daily tests, standardised spelling tests, or a mix and match of assessment strategies?

6. What is done about incorrect spellings? Are priority spellings indicated to the pupil, or are none pointed out but a note made elsewhere?

7. At what stage are children taught to use wordbooks and dictionaries? English in the National Curriculum for Key Stage 1 Writing) states, '. . . pupils should be accumulating a bank of words they can spell . . . taught to check spellings and meanings . . . using dictionaries . . .'(DfE 1995) The NLS Framework includes dictionary work from Year 2. Does the policy allow for children to access appropriate dictionaries as soon as they are ready?

### *Spelling difficulties*

Severe spelling problems constrain any attempts to write, forming a barrier, limiting motivation and overshadowing other aspects of writing at which the child may be competent. A spelling policy for all will address spelling difficulties as a matter of priority before they have a negative effect on other writing skills. The policy statement may include the following:

- ensuring letter problems are identified immediately;
- ensuring spelling is linked with handwriting;
- prioritising and justifying words to be learned, e.g. should words like 'hippopotamus' be on spelling lists? and
- implementing long-term strategies to address severe spelling difficulties through a child's primary years.

If the spelling difficulty is severe, a child needs survival strategies to cope with it. Severe spelling problems need a long-term plan that is operational for as long as necessary – for some poor spellers, this may mean throughout primary school. A policy for implementing long-term spelling strategies could be part of a child's IEP and could include the following:

- a named person to coordinate the spelling strategy;
- discussion with the pupil, parents and other relevant staff to ensure shared understanding of how the policy operates;
- the pupil taking responsibility for his own coping strategies, with adult support;
- prioritising words to be learned and sticking to them;
- stating the pupil's learning strategies and teaching him how to apply them;
- ensuring a consistent support network;
- setting aside 'catch-up' time as part of the plan; and
- stating in writing how the home and school elements of the spelling strategy should be compatible.

A policy for addressing difficulties early, continuously and consistently will minimise the effects of spelling problems on other areas of learning.

### *Standard English*

The general requirements for English in the National Curriculum state that, 'standard English is distinguished from other forms of English by its vocabulary . . . rules and conventions of grammar, spelling and punctuation'. Formal writing is often judged by its adherence to standard English. Getting a job may depend upon a firm grip of standard English. There is no doubt that both are essential to reading and writing development.

Approaches to the use of standard English should consider those children whose speech may not conform to grammatical conventions. The speaking skills of many children for whom English is a second language often reflect the language they hear in the playground, and develop as a colloquial representation of English: standard English writing has to be specifically taught. Dialect differences may account for what appears to be poor attention to grammar. Sensitive discussion of dialect within the context of differences between spoken and written English can help to prevent children from feeling that their speech is inferior. The policy needs to promote the principle that the term 'standard' is not always equated with 'correct'.

The need to perfect grammar presents dire problems for some learners with SEN. Alston (1995) reminds us that, 'grammatical skills tend to develop . . . from the spoken word . . . many less able pupils write as they speak for a longer period than their peers'. The comparison of spoken and written sentences is an ongoing need for children who struggle in this area. Sentence work in the literacy hour will help to address such problems, but the key points will need to be reinforced for less able children. This is best done in groups, with lots of talk. Two points are central:

- explicit teaching of standard English grammar needs to be part of a whole-school policy, sensitive to appropriate contexts and stages of development for all pupils; and
- standard English is only one form of English: there is no right or wrong.

Clearly, if spoken and written standard English act as a currency and a judgement within certain areas of society, children need to be taught to use it appropriately.

### *Marking policy*

No writing policy can be complete without a section on marking, since progression for all learners depends on how writing is monitored, assessed and developed consistently. Marking is more fully addressed in Chapter 11.

## Roles and responsibilities for writing

Raised standards for all children depend on clear roles and responsibilities. The clarification of who does what and when relies on a coordinated approach to addressing writing difficulties. How far professionals and parents contribute to the writing team is a crucial success factor for children with SEN. The following questions may stimulate debate:

- who takes overall responsibility for the writing policy?
- who is responsible for the SEN section?
- who is responsible for writing policy relating to specific areas of SEN, e.g. a long-term spelling plan, addressing dyspraxia problems, or SpLD?

There are no easy answers to the above questions. If a large majority of children with learning difficulties are to be included in the drive to raise standards through the NLS, then key players need to work in tandem. These questions raise issues for staff discussion which apply to all areas of literacy. The following adults are all involved in literacy to some extent: Literacy Governor, head teacher, Literacy Coordinator, SENCO, SEN specialist, class teacher, SEN support assistants and parents. Responsibilities for writing are addressed in Chapter 10, from the perspective of using support staff.

Clearly the Literacy Governor and head teacher are central to the success of all school policy. The Literacy Coordinator may be responsible for the writing policy, but at which point does it overlap with that of the SEN policy? A policy for all recognises a team approach towards Code of Practice and NLS requirements and states how its members will work together to raise writing standards.

Pupils also have responsibilities. Procedures which promote learners as part of the writing team help to ensure success, especially for children with writing difficulties.

### Links with other policies

The writing policy should state how it relates to other key policies, e.g. parental partnership, use of support staff and assessment.

### Policy evaluation

The effectiveness of the writing policy needs to be evaluated. Assuming that children's progress in writing acts as the main indicator of policy performance, the key question is how progress will be observed, monitored and recorded. Is there to be a portfolio of writing samples at each National Curriculum level to ensure consistency? Are samples of individual pupils' writing collated and filed over time to provide evidence of progress, and allow the success of the writing policy to be judged? Chapter 11 explores strategies for assessing writing, with further suggestions for inclusion in the writing policy.

## *The NLS – a long-term literacy plan*

Policy leads to effective planning. The NLS has provided a national scheme of work for literacy which states what pupils should be taught. The school policy for reading and writing enables the termly NLS objectives to be converted into appropriate teaching units, unique for each school. One departure from the traditional content for teaching literacy is the equal balance of fiction and non-fiction for both reading and writing.

### Balancing fiction and non-fiction

Consider the examples of non-fiction writing listed below. From their reception year, children have to understand print, and through composition:

- write their own name;
- write labels;
- write sentences to match pictures . . .



Reception pupils are to 'use writing to discuss' and 'to communicate'.

From Year 1, the use of strategy is important as pupils are to 'apply phonological, graphic knowledge and sight vocabulary to spell words accurately'. This strategy is to be reinforced throughout Key Stage 1. By the end of Year 1 children should also have been taught to write simple recounts (e.g. about a school trip); write own questions prior to reading for information; write labels and extended captions; and make simple lists for planning and reminding.

By the end of Year 2, non-fiction writing will have included writing simple instructions, with diagrams as necessary; making simple notes from non-fiction texts; writing non-fiction texts; and writing non-chronological reports.

By the end of Key Stage 1 children will have already been introduced to a range of non-fiction as well as the more traditional stories and poems.

By the end of Year 3, non-fiction writing has included writing letters, notes and messages. By the end of Year 4, children will also have designed an advertisement; and practised summarising points of view.

By the end of Year 5, children should be able to construct an argument to persuade others, and write a commentary, justifying a personal point of view.

By Year 6 non-fiction writing has included autobiographical writing, e.g. a CV, and writing a balanced report on a controversial issue.

The emphasis on non-fiction reflects the growing recognition that writing consists of far more than stories and poems, and carries implications for school writing policy.

## Policy and the medium-term plan

The medium-term plan sequences termly NLS objectives into manageable teaching units and ensures that:

- work for each year group achieves balance and maintains continuity and progression over time;
- the content of work for parallel classes is consistent; and
- the range of pupil abilities are catered for.

The NLS Framework recognises the problems of planning for mixed-year classes and small schools, and has issued additional guidance for covering NLS objectives on a rolling programme, dependent upon the organisation of the school. This rolling programme may need to stretch forwards and backwards to balance out objectives throughout the key stage.

Planning for classes with a particularly broad range of pupil ability may suggest the need to stretch NLS content in order to take account of pupils at either end of the spectrum. The NLS Framework offers scope for revisiting and revising to secure learning for less able pupils, so catch-up activities need to be included within the medium-term plan.

### *The short-term plan*

The short-term plan breaks down NLS termly objectives into weekly and daily plans, and identifies the differentiation strategies and resources for delivery.

This chapter has opened up a number of policy and planning issues, many of which are expanded in later chapters. If writing is a communicative act, then the aim of the policy must be for all children to communicate effectively in writing to their chosen readers.

*Chapter 5*

# Writing in the Literacy Hour

The literacy hour is the pivot around which the NLS is structured and the major focus for teaching reading and writing. However, it is important to consider the time lapse between what is taught and what is eventually learned, mastered and secured: remember the time-honoured message of Vygotsky that what a child can do with help today, he will do independently tomorrow. Figure 5.1 illustrates three stages of learning, which could usefully be applied to the process of writing.

| Learning stage | The teacher's role |
| --- | --- |
| presentation | sharing different models of writing with pupils at word, sentence and text levels with interactive discussion |
| practice | guiding pupils' practice of writing in the literacy hour, and in subject writing, possibly through writing frames |
| communication | providing opportunities for pupils to communicate to a range of real audiences, for genuine and different purposes, using a broad range of text types |

**Figure 5.1** Stages of learning – the teacher's role

While the literacy hour places a set time and focus on the presentation elements of learning, and some of the practice, much further practice is needed by most children before they can communicate effectively in writing. Chapter 9 expands on cross-curricular writing as the broader context of the NLS and explores the range of text types or genres.

## *Writing in and out of the literacy hour*

Not all school writing will fit into the literacy hour: Figure 5.2 illustrates possible writing activities in and out of the hour.

This chapter is concerned with what takes place in the literacy hour. Further chapters consider writing outside the hour.

### Allocating writing time

Time for writing in the literacy hour is a prior consideration if children are to practice writing a range of text types, each requiring differing amounts of time. In addition, children need greater or lesser amounts of time to complete a piece of writing properly. Many types of writing intended for an audience go through a revision process before they emerge as the final product. Key skills in writing at Key Stage 2 state that, 'children should be taught to write in response to more demanding tasks', and they should be given opportunities to 'plan, draft and improve their work on paper and on screen'(p15, English in the National Curriculum; DfE 1995).

| Writing opportunities | In the hour | Out of the hour |
|---|---|---|
| shared writing | ✓ | |
| guided writing | ✓ | |
| independent writing activities | ✓ | ✓ |
| subject writing | ✓ | ✓ |
| display writing | | ✓ |
| incidental writing | | ✓ |
| free choice writing | ✓ | ✓ |

**Figure 5.2** Writing in and out of the literacy hour

To develop their writing children should be taught to, and have allocated time to:

- plan writing – note and develop initial ideas;
- structure a first draft from the initial ideas;
- revise the first draft to improve shape and form;
- proof-read – to detect spelling, punctuation and sentence errors; and
- present – prepare a final neat copy, on paper or screen.

Children need to move confidently between text, sentence and word level as they go through the above process to produce a final piece of writing with which they feel a sense of achievement. Of course, not all writing needs to go through the above process. Many very short text types may fit into the time-scale of the literacy hour. Consider the following examples from the NLS Framework:

- write labels and captions (Reception);
- make simple lists (Year 1, Term 1);
- write own questions prior to reading for information (Year 1, Term 3);
- to produce simple flowcharts or diagrams (Year 2, Term 2);
- to write metaphors . . . from own ideas or from similes (Year 5, Term 1);
- to write a brief synopsis of a text, e.g. blurb (Year 6, Term 3).

The objectives for fiction and poetry composition tend to need greater allocations of time. Most objectives needing less time tend to be in the non-fiction category. The problem of allocating time for writing is alleviated partly by balancing brief objectives with those requiring extended time at the medium-term planning stage.

## The problem of unfinished writing

The issue of time is important as nothing is more frustrating for pupils and teachers than pages of incomplete work. A child with writing problems who has genuinely tried to produce a good piece of writing will be less likely to repeat the effort if he cannot finish it.

If the aim is for pupils to learn how to process writing towards a finished product, then process time needs to be adequate for all learners. A further problem is that writing cannot be assessed if it is incomplete. The need for time often conflicts with the need to bring some degree of rigour to the teaching and learning of literacy. The problem may be alleviated by the following:

- explaining to all pupils the importance of time;
- using a kitchen timer or clock with movable hands to indicate the amount of time available;
- reminding pupils when they have only five minutes left;
- ensuring that time allocated for each objective is realistic for all pupils; and
- planning some time each week for the completion of written work, especially where pupils have shown enthusiasm for a particular text type.

This problem may also be alleviated by using the fifth literacy hour of the week now and again as an extended writing workshop. The literacy hour is not intended as the only focused time for the teaching of English, and five literacy hours per week is likely to be less than the allocation for English prior to the NLS Framework being introduced.

### From word to text level

The structure of the literacy hour creates a vital link between the parts of writing taught as skills and strategies, and the context in which they are used to enhance learning. All children need to see writing modelled from its whole context and to appreciate where the part they are working on fits in. For example, where lists of spellings are taught, children need to see the spellings in books, and lessons on punctuation need to start from seeing punctuation in fiction and non-fiction texts. Shared reading and writing allows children to experience the whole text before they work on its parts.

The principle of linking skills with their context applies to composition, as well as word work. Children may be working on story beginnings as part of their medium-term input on fiction. If examples of story openings have featured as the shared reading, the class could compose only opening sentences or paragraphs to illustrate reading 'hooks' as an alternative to a complete story.

## *Writing in the literacy hour*

Given that not all writing can be fitted into the hour, what role does writing play in the literacy hour, and how does it support writing across the rest of the curriculum? The function of writing in the literacy hour is to teach children how to write, focusing on modelling text types, offering learners explicit instruction on how to produce the different types of writing, and guiding their practice.

### Modelling writing

If children are to develop into mature writers they must have opportunities to see what good writing looks like. Modelling writing means showing learners different types of writing for them to use as models, and talking about the different attributes of each type. Consider the Year 1, Term 1 NLS objective 'to make simple lists for planning and reminding'. Modelling a list may involve:

- showing children different kinds of lists;
- talking about why they are lists, i.e. words or phrases are written underneath each other;
- explaining that there is no need for full stops as they are not sentences; or
- talking about the purpose of lists as reminders, e.g. a list for the supermarket or a Christmas shopping list.

Consider the NLS objective to 'write own playscript' (Year 5, Term 1). Modelling playscripts in preparation for writing them could include:

- showing children a range of playscripts;
- reading plays together during shared reading;

- talking about what a play is;
- talking about why a playscript is composed of dialogue;
- talking about why space is left at the side of each page for the producer to make notes; or
- talking about the stage directions and the narrator's role.

Children with learning difficulties will benefit a great deal from explicit modelling and instruction on writing. Models for writing are further expanded in Chapter 8.

## Using a writing frame

Lewis and Wray (1998) describe the writing frame as a means of 'introducing children to different written genres and then supporting them in the use of appropriate text structures.' Writing frames can be used to guide both fiction and non-fiction writing, providing a skeleton outline for a piece of writing around which children structure their own ideas. Figure 5.3 illustrates a frame to guide the writing of an informal letter to a friend, the purpose of which is to help stimulate ideas for children who find it difficult to generate their own.

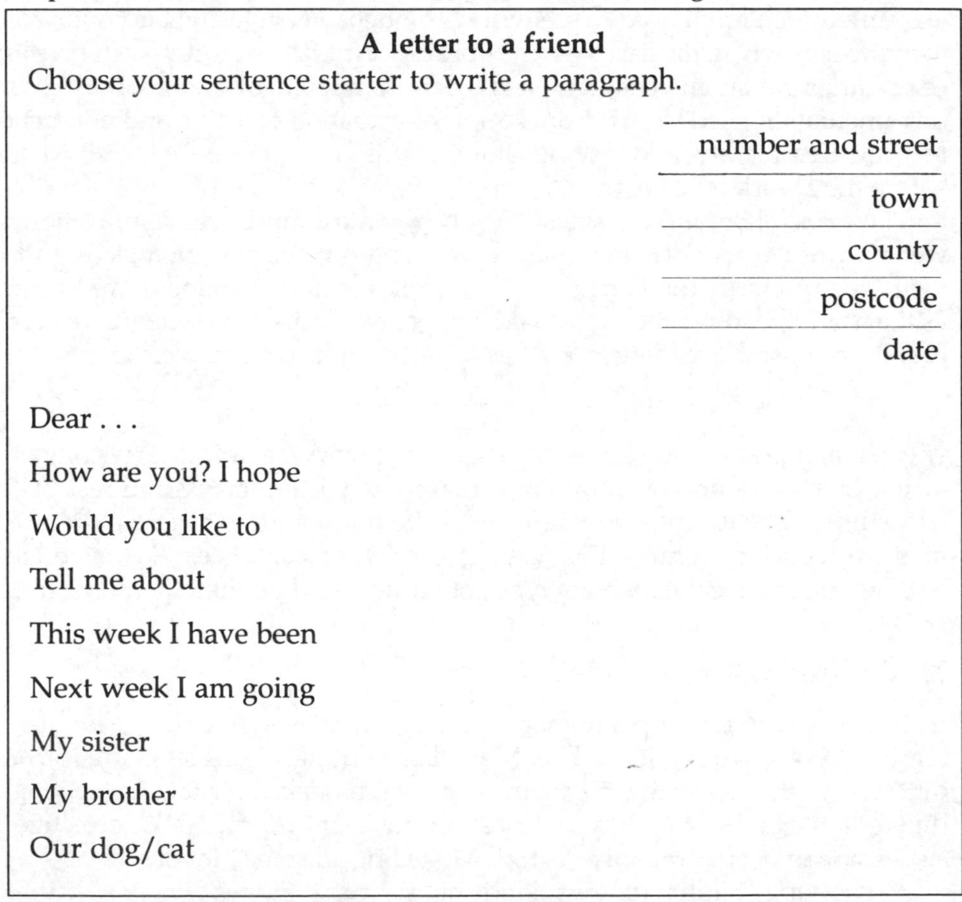

**A letter to a friend**

Choose your sentence starter to write a paragraph.

number and street

town

county

postcode

date

Dear . . .

How are you? I hope

Would you like to

Tell me about

This week I have been

Next week I am going

My sister

My brother

Our dog/cat

**Figure 5.3** A sample frame for an informal letter

The writing frame provides the scaffolding around which children shape their thoughts. As authors often lament, nothing is worse than a blank page. Many children with SEN fail to write because they cannot get their initial thoughts down on paper. By using a frame, most children can 'fill in' between the frames and produce a piece of writing.

However, writing frames need to be carefully used. All children have to read the words which form the frame in order to use it independently. How much framing do children need? Some less able children may need frames which provide a little more scaffolding and less empty space to fill in, as a step towards a more minimal writing frame. On the other hand, scaffolding should prompt children to write without stifling their creativity. The vocabulary of writing frames needs to be talked about with children before they write, as phrases such as 'with reference to' or 'notwithstanding' are not part of children's natural language. Part of the function of writing frames is to expand children's use of appropriate connective language.

Writing frames have potential provided that all learners are shown how to use them as stepping stones towards independence. They are a valuable resource, but care must be taken not to allow the frames to lead the planning. The use of frames should allow a common topic to become an individual writing experience for all learners.

## Balancing continuous and blocked objectives

Writing in the literacy hour will include both blocked and continuous work: blocked work is mainly composition. Objectives are blocked in for teaching during particular weeks, possibly revisited and secured at a later stage, then left to be practised and monitored through cross-curricular writing. Continuous work is more likely to be at word and sentence level and includes focused attention to spelling, handwriting, punctuation and sentence construction. Much of this work will emanate from shared reading and writing in the hour. The word work should also reflect pupils' IEPs and present opportunities for work on specific targets.

Explicit teaching as a whole class offers less able pupils the chance to demonstrate their achievement in writing composition, provided that the barriers of spelling, handwriting and punctuation are not allowed to get in the way. Consider how far the following NLS objectives can be accessed by all children at their own level:

- to write stories using simple settings (Year 1, Term 3);
- to write simple instructions (Year 2, Term 1);
- to write simple playscripts (Year 3, Term 1);
- to write character sketches (Year 4, Term 1) (NLS Framework, DfEE 1998).

### *Providing focus and balance*

Less able writers are often overwhelmed by their problems. As barriers of spelling, handwriting and sentence structure interfere with the creativity of writing, children have too much to think about and very little writing is produced: this problem is enlarged when the task is an extended piece of writing. The following suggestions may help pupils to retain a clear focus:

- clarify the outcome for learners. If the shape and form of a letter, or a set of instructions, is the objective then focus attention on that outcome.
- remove spelling and handwriting as interference problems. Separate them from the objectives of writing composition. Keep separate sessions for focusing on spelling and handwriting.
- ensure the feedback to learners reflects the writing objective.

Learners with a long-term spelling problem may be inspired to write an extended piece if freed from their spelling prison. Their spelling plan would then operate alongside composition writing and be informed by it — it is not suggested that spelling and handwriting are ignored. If children have demonstrated certain spelling knowledge during focused sessions, then they should be encouraged to apply their knowledge to composition. Proof-reading should focus on what the writer knows, and lead to progression: if children have reached the cursive handwriting stage during focused sessions, there is no excuse for untidy printing during writing composition.

The suggestion is not to minimise problems associated with spelling and handwriting, as these form the cornerstones of writing. However, many learners never move beyond those difficulties if they are allowed to interfere with every other aspect of writing. Where learners demonstrate multi-dimensional and acute writing difficulties, only a sensitive and prioritised approach can help them move forward.

## Vocabulary extension in the literacy hour

Vocabulary work is a vital element of the NLS Framework. From reception children are taught to:

- use new words from their reading and shared experiences;
- make collections of personal interest or significant words linked to particular topics.

From Year 1, they are also to:

- use the terms 'vowel' and 'consonant'; and from Year 2, to:
- use antonyms, discuss differences of meaning and their spelling;
- use synonyms and other alternative words/phrases that express the same or similar meanings.

From Year 3, as well as expanding vocabulary, they are to improve the precision of their writing by the use of vocabulary that is appropriate for its purpose. Throughout Key Stage 2, the focus of vocabulary work is on being able to use the right word in the right place, and to understand how the use of particular words can bring subtle nuances and shades of meaning to text. Vocabulary work is a vital element of the NLS for all children. Restricted vocabulary strips writing of its clarity, precision and vividness. Vocabulary work has three elements:

1. expanding children's knowledge of vocabulary;
2. improving the precision of vocabulary, and leading children away from generalised words, e.g. big and nice;
3. enriching vocabulary where particular nuances of meaning are needed to give mood or atmosphere to a written piece.

Activities for vocabulary work could include the following:

- taking basic words such as 'big' and making a list of synonyms, e.g. immense, large, huge, enormous, magnificent;
- placing different nouns with the adjectives generated and discussing which pairs create the best rhythmic match — enormous dinosaur, huge dinosaur;
- working on the development of root words - care, careful, careless, carelessness, caring;
- discussing the meanings of common prefixes and suffixes: fore-, dis-, mal-, -ful, -ology;
- discussing shades of meaning in synonyms — tasty, fruity, luscious, juicy, tangy;
- debating the use of two or three possible words to fit into a sentence during shared writing, and discussing the reasons why one particular word is better than another;
- classifying words in categories and sub-categories, e.g. fruits, animals, clothes, summer fruits, wild or domestic animals, holiday or work clothes;
- gathering sets of words that are particularly interesting, evoke colourful images, suggest vitality, or are warm and pleasant;
- listing vocabulary from shared reading to demonstrate a particular atmosphere from the text and adding others; or

- selecting interesting or important words from what is read and talking about their precise function in the text. Are they developing character? Are they adding to the atmosphere? Are they providing mystery?

*SEN issues*

Focused vocabulary work benefits all children, and activities such as those listed above help to develop spoken language as well as reading and writing. The value of vocabulary work stems from interactive discussion. It is important that all children fully understand the meaning of new words before they are asked to read or write them.

Vocabulary work may encourage 'safe-spellers' to try new words. When vocabulary has been talked about, children could be asked to think how the words could possibly be spelt. Is a word short or long? What is its first sound? What about its final sound? The syllables could be clapped to aid the thinking process; children may need to be reminded of the grapheme choices for the phonemes they are hearing.

Encouraging all children to join in may lead some to using more adventurous vocabulary in their writing in the knowledge that trying to spell new words is the way to improve spelling skills. They need to know that they are not expected to get it exactly right the first time.

New vocabulary could be displayed over the course of the week and reinforced during odd moments – at some point each day children could talk about a word on display for two or three minutes. A multi-sensory approach to learning new vocabulary will help all children to retain it: work on food words may involve tasting, or a 'feely' bag can help children to focus on words of touch – rough, smooth, prickly, bumpy. Developing vocabulary through the senses helps children to assimilate it in a meaningful way.

## Shared writing

'Two heads are better than one' is an old cliché given fresh significance for the literacy hour. Writing has traditionally been a solitary activity. Professional writers write in isolation. The idea of children sharing writing is based on the known benefits of talking about it and explicitly teaching it. NLS Framework training Module 1 reminds teachers of the main features of shared writing:

- the teacher may model aspects of writing using children's own contributions;
- the teacher and children collaborate to plan and develop a piece of writing together;
- teaching may focus upon the structure and content of different text types;
- shared writing is linked to reading.

Iverson and Reeder (1998) describe shared writing as the mirror to shared reading, allowing children to participate in producing a message they would be unable to do alone. Unlike its mirror image, shared writing is often part of the dual experience of modelling a particular text type, prior to writing a class version together. For example, in order to write a recount of a school outing to a museum, children must have read other recounts with the teacher to see how they are structured.

While reading and writing provide a dual learning experience, assessment necessarily separates the skills and strategies for each area of literacy. Lesson plans must clearly indicate which NLS objectives act as the main focus of the instruction.

Many reading objectives will involve writing as part of the focused activity: children may be using letter cubes to make CVC words, spelling them to aid the skill of reading them. Conversely, writing objectives will involve reading as the modelling element of the writing activity.

Shared writing from the reading model could provide 'home-made' texts written by children for the following day's shared reading experience, which is a further example of reading and writing feeding each other with resources as well as joint literacy experiences for learners.

Shared, interactive writing in the literacy hour offers all children, including those with writing difficulties, opportunities to do the following:

- contribute to a group writing experience;
- learn about different types of texts;
- learn how to apply known writing skills and strategies;
- develop their writing vocabulary;
- learn the skills of spelling, handwriting and punctuation; and
- learn how to use people, ICT and other support in order to become independent in writing.

Children with learning difficulties will benefit from seeing good writing modelled and talking about what makes an effective piece of communication: what is it that makes writing good or better?

Redfern and Edwards (1997) argue the case for modelling as the way forward. 'As the teacher models the craft of writing . . . judicial comments help children move from implicit to explicit knowledge about the writing process. Crossings out can be made, additions inserted . . . dialogue perfected.' The authors' comments are made in the context of practical ways to inspire young authors, but apply to all types of writing. It is particularly important for children with SEN to see the process of drafting, crossings out and all. Given that the objective is to improve children's writing, all pupils need to be taught what 'better' writing is and to be shown how they can achieve it.

## Guided writing

Guided writing differs from shared writing as learners move from modelling, discussion and joint composition to the task of producing their own writing under controlled conditions. Guided writing is half-way between shared and independent writing, and is intended to develop writing skills while ensuring support and success for all children. The NLS Framework training unit Module 1 describes the main features of guided writing as:

- children are placed in small groups according to writing ability;
- the focus is on a specific, challenging aspect of writing;
- children work on individual pieces of writing, often linked to their reading, using the knowledge acquired from word and sentence level work;
- the teacher focuses on children's skills;
- the teacher gives explicit feedback and points the way forward.

During guided writing all children receive focused attention on how to improve their skills, and because children are in ability groups this allows the teacher to attend to writing difficulties and lead children forward from their starting point. As Iverson and Reeder (1998) point out, guided writing offers children opportunities to develop the range of writing skills and strategies as they are taught to:

- shape their thoughts into written form;
- produce messages in a variety of genres;
- master letter formation;
- hear and record sounds in unknown words;
- spell high frequency words;
- make analogies to spell new words; and
- develop their use of punctuation.

## Independent activities

Shared and guided writing in the literacy hour is part of the process towards independent writing in other areas of the curriculum. Writing independence can be considered in two ways: as the activity of writing without assistance from a teacher, i.e. the process; and as the gradual acquisition of writing skills and strategies i.e. the outcome.

Independence matures through the process of working on writing independently. All children have to be self-reliant so that guided writing can take place with different groups, and children with SEN must learn to work for twenty minutes without teacher guidance. The following chapter offers suggestions for developing the ability of all children to work independently.

## *Progression in writing*

Progression depends on a careful balance of shared, guided and independent writing activities with opportunities for learners to reinforce literacy hour teaching through their writing in other subjects. The aim is for children to move gradually from using a writing frame as a scaffold towards writing independently from their own confidence, skills and knowledge. Figure 5.4 summarises the stages towards writing independence.

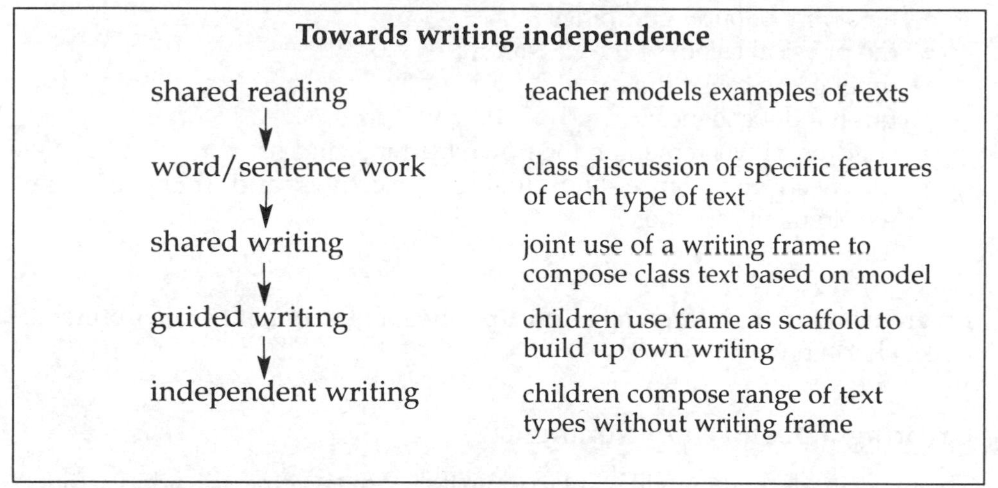


**Figure 5.4** Towards writing independence

It will take time to refine the literacy hour structure in order for all pupils and adults to gain maximum benefit. The following positive comments have been made by teachers from their experiences of the literacy hour:

- we are paying more focused attention to texts;
- we are talking a lot more about words;
- the hour seems to have a competitive element;
- children are really thinking about reading and writing;
- modelling different texts is extending children's views of literacy;
- I am getting to know each child's skill levels more;
- higher order literacy skills are receiving more attention;
- children like the big books for science and history.

Few professionals would disagree with the philosophy and principles of teaching literacy through a focused and well-structured approach. Progression for all children, including those with SEN, and able pupils, depends on careful organisation.

*Chapter 6*

# Organising Practical Writing Activities

Organising writing within the context of literacy and the wider curriculum combines many of the issues raised so far and reflects the philosophy and principles of the writing policy. Getting all of the elements working well together depends on key sections operating as smoothly as a symphony orchestra with the teacher as the conductor. Organisation may be influenced by the following factors:

- the need to differentiate for the range of pupils;
- range of SEN;
- writing environment;
- the deployment of human and material resources;
- flexibility of pupil groupings;
- the physical layout of the classroom;
- timetabling constraints;
- pupil independence;
- children's involvement in their own learning; and
- the need to balance NLS literacy objectives and their differing requirements of time.

## *The writing environment*

Progression for all children relies on a positive and stimulating environment: make children want to write!

### Creating a positive environment

The majority of children will want to write if they see writing as a good activity with useful and pleasurable spin-offs. Writing problems are minimised in an environment which:

- respects every learner's personal best;
- teaches all children to accept diversity;
- has high expectations for all learners, but sets realistic goals which individuals can reach;
- recognises small steps of progress;
- encourages healthy competition built upon mutual trust;
- believes that success is founded on the notion that written work is never wrong, but can always be improved.

A positive atmosphere depends on children feeling relaxed about their writing. Children with SEN need to feel confident that they will get there, however long it takes, and that people are there to support them. Many less able writers lose the heart to try, when their own writing efforts fail to match up with those of peers or the models presented during shared reading and writing. All children need to see the learning process and to know that the finished product takes many years to achieve.

Less able writers will gain confidence if time and space are created for them to write from choice as well as from direction. If confidence is the aim, inform children when they can write. A positive environment needs to be age-appropriate, so a writing table could be available with different colours and textures of writing paper (from firms and the community), and pencils, pens, crayons, markers, and so on could be provided as appropriate to stimulate the activity of writing as an enjoyable activity.

## Using writing models

As writing assumes a more serious purpose, the writing table may require models for reference. Different examples of text types could be displayed, or kept in a book for easy access by all children. Collecting examples of writing for a 'models book' will never be a problem, since pupils will delight in finding a range of texts. Discussion of what children bring in could result in highlighting and labelling the key features of each text type before it is put into the models book, to aid pupils' independence in using it. The collective effort will stimulate discussion about text types and promote literacy as part of the link between home and school.

## Exemplifying reality

If children are to approach tasks with enthusiasm and vigour, any perception that writing is for the teacher to assess must be removed. Writing is rooted in reality: how can school writing become a genuine act of communication for children, allowing them to practise their skills on real readers, and receive a response?

Schools may benefit from looking at writing from a different perspective and questioning how much of the writing that takes place in school could be done by children, with a little adult support as necessary. At any time there will be a list of jobs waiting. Consider the following:

- labels for cupboards around the school;
- display captions for artwork in the hall;
- a heading and a joint conclusion for science graphs in the classroom;
- a poster for the forthcoming school craft fair;
- a 'thank-you' letter to the caretaker for putting up the new shelves in the classroom;
- a reference guide for the library showing children how the non-fiction sections are coded;
- notices to inform parents and visitors where to go on parents' evenings or open days; or
- letters to local businesses requesting samples of different writing paper for the writing table.

The final products may be less neat and precise than those written by teachers, but where parents and the community are educated to see the benefits of the real approach, they will appreciate writing development in progress. A further benefit will be community links with schools. Children having a genuine role in school writing helps to promote joint effort and motivation from children at every ability level, provided that individual contributions are sensitively treated. Figure 6.1 illustrates a 'writing task book' into which jobs can be entered by children or adults as they arise, and attended to during planned or free writing time.

Bringing reality to school writing encourages all children to enter into the spirit of learning when the focus is less on perfection and more on process and the individual's best efforts. Less able writers will be stimulated by seeing their work on the wall or by receiving a real response to their communication.

The real writing approach needs clear understanding by pupils of how the system will work. Children could be assigned, or could choose, to work on a writing job. If names are entered, the book provides a record of what writing has been done, and by whom, as part of the evidence base for assessment.

First drafts could be presented to the whole class for 'consultation' prior to the group redrafting, e.g. if a group have written a letter on behalf of the class.

| Writing task book Class: AY | | |
|---|---|---|
| **Job waiting** | **Date done** | **Writing group** |
| labels for cupboard | 10th Feb | Tom Pat Emma |
| letter to paper firm | 12th Feb | Jane Paul |
| list of books needing repair | | |
| article for newsletter | | |

**Figure 6.1** Sample of a writing task book

### Routines for writing

The writing environment will benefit from routines which are clarified between adults and pupils. For example:

- are children expected to write every day whether they feel like it or not?
- who is to read the writing and what outcome can the writer expect for his or her efforts?
- how will free-choice writing and assigned writing sit compatibly together?
- how and when will a writing task which focuses on parts (e.g. the first paragraph of a story) be related to its whole context?
- how can continuous work, e.g. on spelling and handwriting, progress alongside blocked work, e.g. the NLS Framework objectives for composition?
- how are longer and shorter writing tasks to be organised?
- how can individual children's long-term spelling or handwriting plans be accommodated into medium- and short-term planning?

## *Classroom layout*

A positive writing environment enables independence. Children need to assemble their tools, and be able to find information, without asking adults or peers. Consideration of classroom layout may include:

- where key features of the writing environment are to be placed, e.g. the writing table;
- how children are to independently access tools and information;
- how flexible pupil groupings are to be accommodated;
- the computer and Language Master are to be safe and accessible without being noise distractions for children working on other tasks;
- where display can be most effective.

The above points open out many issues concerning the writing environment. While the size and shape of classrooms may be constant, the flexibility of desk arrangements and display areas can help to maximise literacy potential.

### Writing displays

How writing is displayed will have a marked effect on its usefulness. Writing display could include models to support the writing process and a writing wall for the display of work in process, as well as displays of completed and polished pieces of work.

Models to support the writing process are there to remind all children what they are aiming towards. The focus of this part of display could be for the writing models which feature on the current medium-term plan. During the time-scale of the plan, the writing models are for reference and as visual aids to discussion, after which they could be filed in the models book by the writing table to support independent writing tasks as necessary.

The writing wall could be simply an assigned area for pieces of writing done during the week. Pupils place their work on the writing wall (having got out blu-tack by themselves). By Friday an assortment of writing tasks will be evident, some of which will have emanated from the reading objectives, strengthening children's perceptions of reading and writing together.

The display of completed and polished writing needs to reflect all abilities, yet model certain features of 'good' writing. One solution, to include children with SEN, is to have a shared understanding from all children that 'good' represents a personal best. The polished pieces then reflect not the best writers in the class but those pieces which demonstrate a great deal of effort and attention to the main points of the instruction, regardless of writing conventions under development, e.g. children with a long-term spelling plan. The spelling should at least represent a child's personal best with regard to their progress on their plan.

Children with SEN are less likely to be embarrassed about their spelling being seen by others if the clear message from teachers is that what is on the wall represents good work on an aspect of composition. This could be effective opening sentences for a story, or instructions showing good layout: a caption could state the objective of the work. A sensitive approach and acceptance of diversity will help to promote openness and sharing of writing.

Each display has a function. Where it is placed, and how children perceive it, will enhance or reduce its impact. Displays often appear to be more directed towards parents and visitors than to their writers. These points may help to stimulate debate on how displays can be most effective:

- are items at the right height for children to read?
- what about different fonts, capital and lower case lettering and sectioning of the display? If children see the impact of different writing techniques they are more likely to emulate them.
- does the display invite responses? A range of sentences, i.e. statements, instructions and questions can help to make displays interactive and help children to understand the function of different kinds of sentences.

Displays offer a powerful extension to the focused teaching of reading and writing. Advertising creates a great deal of impact on readers from minimal input. Displays which advertise key points from what is taught and promote the principles of the writing policy will enhance learning.

## Writing tools and reference sources

For all children to be independent, particularly during the literacy hour, they must know what is theirs to use. While the labelling of tools and resources needs to be age-appropriate, it helps groups to be self-organising: if colour is the coding system, the blue group know that what is blue belongs to their table. Pencils, rubbers and even dictionaries could be assigned to tables with responsibility for groups to take care of their own tools.

## *Developing writing independence*

The NLS suggests that it is important to encourage pupils' independence in order to allow children to develop and apply autonomous learning strategies to their own reading and writing; and to allow the teacher to focus on guided reading and writing by reducing dependency on the teacher. (p15, National Literacy Strategy, Training Module 1; DfEE 1998.)

Independence is an essential aim for all children including those with SEN as far as their learning difficulty allows. Pupils' attitudes towards independence and their skills need to be trained as well as encouraged. In the context of the literacy hour, with the focus on writing, it is important to achieve both writing and working independence. Each enriches the other, yet relies on a distinct set of skills. Pupils' abilities to develop writing independence rely upon their attitudes to working independently.

## Working independence

Consider how far each of the following contributes to independent working:

- ability to be a member of different peer groups;
- ability to remain on task for directed lengths of time;
- ability to cope with changes of task in lessons;
- ability to handle movement within lessons;
- ability to make activity choices as appropriate;
- ability to move between tasks without teacher direction when appropriate;
- ability to follow a task management board;
- ability to look after own equipment and working tools;
- ability to work on different kinds of tasks and adapt social behaviour accordingly, e.g. switch from a group spelling game to a paired task on redrafting.

The above abilities comprise some of the many areas of working independence which allow pupils to become more self-reliant in reading and writing. All children benefit from focused training on areas such as those listed.

It is often thought that children with SEN cannot work independently, yet many pupils with learning difficulties can develop independence strategies if they are carefully taught and rewarded for the required behaviour. It is easy to smother pupils' efforts towards independence if they have an assigned learning support assistant (LSA) hovering all the time. The LSA who moves sensitively around the class delivering support to pupils as needed, while still focusing on the named child at intervals, can do much to promote working independence for children with SEN. Independence needs to be age-appropriate and starts from a state of mind before it develops into a set of skills. The process starts in the nursery, or reception, where children can be taught how things are to be put away and got out for each task by modelling, coaching and rewarding. Training for such minute aspects of independence may appear simplistic, but is necessary to build up the required attitudes towards self-reliance in children. Persevering until pupils do exactly what is required will initially use precious time, but time spent at the beginning will save more time and energy later on. Movements of task and time during the literacy hour, and other curricular work, will operate more smoothly as children begin to see themselves as part of a collective unit.

Pupil interruptions eat into valuable class time. The NLS has suggested the following common reasons why children interrupt teachers:

- for help with spellings;
- to ask what to do if stuck;
- to access resources;
- to mediate in disagreements with peers;
- they have finished their work;
- for attention. (National Literacy Strategy, Training Module 1: The Literacy Hour; DfEE 1998.)

To minimise the impact of interruptions, show the class how to work from a task management board as a vital first step. Model, coach and reward accordingly: no child should ever be unsure which task to work on next.

Coding resources for each group as suggested earlier in this chapter will promote responsibility for equipment. Showing children exactly where to place different pieces of work, with labels as reminders, will ensure coordination. Try having a group leader, where appropriate, and rotating this responsibility each term or half-term. A chart on the wall could show group leadership roles for:

- getting out, checking and putting away group equipment;
- placing finished work in its designated place;
- briefing the group for working on a joint task; or
- operating ICT equipment when a group is working on it.

Such roles would have to be part of the independence training programme so that children are in no doubt of their responsibility, and arguments about who does what are prevented. If group leader roles are rotated all children can have a turn to lead something and social skills will be greatly enhanced.

A poster on the wall, as illustrated in Figure 6.2, could remind children what to do when 'stuck'.

**What to do if I am stuck!**

Think!

| | | |
|---|---|---|
| What do I need? | – | a spelling? information? equipment? |
| Where can I find it? | – | in the reference area? in the cupboard? from a friend? |
| If I can't find it | – | magic line? spell checker? |

Do another task until the teacher is free.

**Figure 6.2** What to do if 'stuck'

## Writing independence

Many areas listed above relate to writing independence; for example, pupils needing help with spellings. In addition, children need to have clear perceptions of the task they have been asked to do and be able to use reference materials for finding out instead of asking the teacher or peers. Strategies for encouraging writing independence could include:

- having the task clearly stated on the management board or work table to remind children who forget what to do;
- word books for spellings, subject vocabulary lists, dictionaries at the right level etc, so that children can find out rather than ask; and
- instructing children how to use writing frames and ensuring the right level of scaffolding from the writing frame for children of differing abilities.

Figure 6.3 illustrates a task management board for writing composition during independent activities. Children are working on the NLS objective to 'write simple instructions', from Year 2, Term 1. Each pupil knows which group he is in, and the task allocated.

### *The 'own choice' book*

When writing independence is a priority, i.e. during independent activities, the own choice book is a useful strategy. Children could be trained to write in their own choice book at particular times, e.g. if they have finished work early, or if they are still stuck in spite of strategies in place to prevent this. The own choice book is a useful device to ensure that children are always doing something useful. To ensure that own choice books are not abused, e.g. by graffiti, teachers could collect them in now and again and reward sensible choices. Pupils need to know that the own choice book is not a scrapbook, and not an excuse for lazy spellings or scruffy writing; nor is it real in the sense of having a genuine audience. Nevertheless, the own choice book provides evidence for assessment. If children know this, they are likely to use it sensibly, sparingly and constructively. Alternatively, own choice time could be directed towards the writing table as children finish early, to form fluid groups for real jobs waiting in the 'writing task book'.

| **Task board** | | **Date** Tuesday 8th December | |
|---|---|---|---|
| **Main objective -** how to write instructions | | | |
| *Group* | *Adult* | *Task* | *Needed for later* |
| Green | | how to play dominoes | Example: Box 2. Card from Drawer 1 |
| Blue | T | how to put P.E. equipment away | Paper: Drawer 3 |
| Yellow | | instructions for paper chains | Coloured paper: Drawer 3 |
| Red | A | making a Father Christmas | Card: Drawer 5<br>Red felt: Drawer 7 |
| Orange | | how to make a Christmas angel | Gold card : 4<br>Bits: Drawer 6 |

**Figure 6.3** Working from a task board

### Pupil ownership and responsibility

Independence depends on pupils knowing where they are going and accepting some responsibility for getting there. Children who know their writing goals are more likely to use own choice books to develop their known targets. Strategies for encouraging pupils to 'own' their writing could include:

- all pupils having writing targets in their books;
- children with IEPs having their targets clearly related to the NLS writing objectives;
- all children being part of the writing team and knowing principles of the writing policy as appropriate, e.g. how different kinds of writing are assessed;
- having a writing checklist for a long-term spelling or handwriting plan, or for the blocked activities of writing composition. Examples of writing checklists are included in Chapter 11.

### Making independence happen

Independence requires trust. It starts from the expectation that all pupils will conform to the required rules, and move between imposed discipline and self-discipline as appropriate. Rewards need a clear indication of what they are for, and good independent behaviour can only follow precise modelling of what is required.

The plenary section of the literacy hour can be used to focus on how various groups have worked and to give positive feedback on working and writing independence. Balancing different activities safely and efficiently relies on all children taking independence seriously as part of their development as readers and writers.

## *Balancing writing activities*

Time does not allow all writing to be taught and practised during the literacy hour, nor do different text types require the same treatment, time, or attention to process. Due consideration to a number of factors may help teachers to organise writing activities.

### Focusing on parts

How far do complete pieces of writing have to be produced within the hour? The main purpose is to show children how to write in the range of text types, i.e. fiction writing has traditionally involved writing a story from beginning to end with due attention to the process of redrafting and copying out ready for presentation. Not all writing has to be a completed text. Though the whole text will be pre-modelled, focused attention on its component parts can illustrate a technique. Activities which focus only on parts of text could include writing opening paragraphs of stories; or writing small sections of dialogue in preparation for writing a playscript.

Purposeful parts of texts are more easily handled during group discussion if time is short, and provide an effective means of focusing on the main teaching points. Working on parts of texts can also help to motivate pupils who dislike having to write extended pieces of writing.

### Length of activities

Not all texts require the same amount of time, nor do they all need to be processed for presentation. Children need time to produce a complete story of two or three sides if the task is to be realistic. On the other hand, the objective of writing simple questions or lists, can be fitted into a twenty minute time slot. Consider the following text types and the amounts of time and attention each one needs: a complete story, a list, a recount of a class outing, a letter to a friend, or brainstorming a topic web for the next history lesson.

A complete story needs the full writing process if quality is desired, since all children need time to produce their best. A simple list may take only minutes and, following a modelling session on different ways to gather ideas, groups may require only minutes to draft out a topic web. Instructions for a game may be a further example of a task which can be completed within the hour, yet allow children the satisfaction of having written a complete text.

### Continuous and blocked writing

How are continuous and blocked activities organised in the hour? When will catch-up sessions be delivered? Continuous activities focus on the skills of spelling, handwriting and sentence structure, which form the conventions of writing and the essence of many pupils' writing difficulties. Blocked activities focus on the NLS objectives for composition taught during particular terms.

The two areas conflict, particularly for children with writing difficulties. Twenty minutes of independent writing will not allow less able pupils to focus on both areas at once. If shape and form are the priority, additional time needs to be planned for work on the conventions of writing, as skills must be regularly practised. Where conventions of writing are the priority, practice of shape and form could be allocated to the wider curriculum. If a clear focus is placed upon the objectives, pupils with writing difficulties know precisely what skills they are concentrating on and do not feel overloaded and anxious.

## *Flexible pupil groupings*

Learning to write involves focused talk through which all children benefit: writing activities should rarely be of a solitary nature. Effective groups help pupils to:

- develop social and communicative skills;
- develop independence;
- develop their skills of collaborative working;
- become better organised; and
- make better progress in reading and writing.

Groups need to be fluid and adaptable, and pupils need to realise why a group is formed and their own role within the group. Adults join a group and participate as members only if they know its purpose and function. Groups may be organised by:

- ability – mainly chosen by the teacher;
- friendship – where pupils choose their own grouping;
- activity – where the activity indicates the group; or
- size – where the number of pupils is the key factor.

If pupils know why a group is formed they will perform better and develop the skills listed above through peer interaction. The following points may help teachers to match activities to different groups, bearing in mind the nature of pupils' writing difficulties.

### A group of one

If children write individually, the purpose should be clearly defined. Assessment is an obvious example of times when children need to demonstrate their skills and strategies. Handwriting may be regarded as a practice activity requiring little talk. If children are to write alone, the task and resources provided have to be accessible for all.

Children may want to write alone, especially if they are afraid to share what they perceive as poor quality. Solitary writing should not be consistently denied, yet it does not help poor writers to improve. Children should be encouraged to enjoy and benefit from collaborative writing.

### Working in pairs

Pair work takes many forms for different purposes. Consider the following activities: redrafting writing; testing spellings; matching jigsaw words or sentences; writing tasks which require pupils to support each other; working on the computer or using a Language Master.

Pair work may be indicated by these activities. Teachers may feel that redrafting lends itself more to working in pairs than in larger groups provided that pairs are well matched. The task of testing spellings is often performed more effectively as pairs, and activities such as matching jigsaw words or sentences may work more effectively in pairs matched by ability so that all children participate. As pairs, children are less likely to 'get lost' and are more likely to contribute to the activity.

### Table-size groups

Some writing activities suggest table-size groups or pairs. Consider how you might group children for the following tasks:

- for story writing, a brainstorming task to collate words which may replace 'said' (exclaimed, muttered, shouted);
- compiling a guidebook for visitors on places to visit in the locality; or
- playing a spelling game.

A brainstorming task requires enough brains to generate ideas. A writing project which is broken down into parts, e.g. producing a guidebook, may start off as a group task. However, the group may split itself into pairs or individuals, and reform as a whole group as necessary throughout the time-scale of the task. A spelling game may require groups of four or six in order for it to work.

It is easy for children with learning difficulties to be in a group without playing an interactive part. Many sit passively, watching rather than participating, if allowed. If groups of more than two are to work effectively in moving all children's writing forward, then all members must contribute.

### Teams

Team work can be an effective means of organising a class and encouraging children to see their role within a larger group. The class could be organised into two teams, each team carefully balanced to include a range of abilities and strengths. The time-scale of the team could match that of the medium-term plan. The function of the team may be to:

- provide a healthy and competitive team spirit;
- improve working and writing independence;
- improve behaviour and enable learning;
- promote collaborative skills; or to
- develop acceptance and tolerance of diversity in terms of ability, race, culture and interests.

Each team will require a leader for the duration of its existence, to be rotated as new teams form. The idea of team and group leadership is far from new but could work effectively in the context of the NLS; for example, groups organised by the teacher for independent activities in the literacy hour could each have a leader as suggested in the independence section. Group leaders may meet each week to talk about how the week has progressed, discuss any problems experienced and how to resolve them. The team leaders could then relay the views of their team to the teacher and raise any issues on behalf of the team. The team approach has potential as children work towards independence in the literacy hour and the NLS in its wider context.

Benefits would be seen in terms of children with SEN developing maturity through team and group approaches; shared responsibilities between pupils, within agreed limits and clearly understood by each child; and the development of a collective identity by pupils.

Some of these suggestions are visionary and far-reaching, as the NLS itself is far-reaching in its expectations for all children, including those with SEN. If the literacy hour is to work, age-appropriate pupil independence is its foundation. Independence cannot happen without flexible and well organised grouping systems.

## *Differentiating writing activities*

The NLS training unit for Module 1 suggests various patterns of organisation for independent work. The unit suggests:

- all of the children . . . on the same task, differentiated by response or outcome;
- a combination of groups working on the same task;
- five groups organised by ability working on differentiated activities;
- four groups organised by ability working on differentiated activities, and the whole class working on the same task on the fifth day (e.g. a piece of extended writing). (National Literacy Strategy, Module 1, Training Materials; DfEE 1998)

It is also suggested that teachers develop their own patterns of organisation. The purpose of this section is to expand on strategies for differentiating writing. Additional guidance to the NLS Framework (DfEE 1998) suggests that, 'By using common texts and activities, teachers can hold the class together, yet maximise participation and challenge children at different levels.' The statement leads directly to the question 'how?'. Differentiating writing stems from knowing children's abilities and needs, and delivering the NLS writing objectives in a way that ensures access for all.

### Differentiating by response or outcome

What kinds of writing tasks suggest differentiation by response or outcome? Tasks may include all children writing a story, or part of it. They may be working on the same NLS objective, e.g. making a list, writing a set of instructions; or writing a playscript.

The same activity can be differentiated by the way in which children are grouped for support. Some may be working individually, while others work in pairs or larger groups. All children can work on the activity of writing a playscript provided they can access the activity, yet the same quality or quantity would not be expected from them all.

### Differentiation by task/activity

Ability groups for independent activities in the literacy hour may suggest differentiation by task/activity, for example:

- work related to children's personal spelling plans;
- phonic work;
- handwriting work at the level required by individual children;
- writing tasks which pick up on children's problems in order to guide writing forward; or
- writing as part of a group or team project, requiring each member to make a different contribution to the outcome.

If children are organised into groups for project work the differentiation would have to take account of what each child (or pair) could contribute. If groups are writing their own non-fiction book, pairs or individuals within the group could, at various stages,be involved in:

- writing the list of contents;
- an introduction;
- researching and writing notes ready for each chapter;
- writing up each chapter;
- writing captions for illustrations;
- drawing the illustrations;
- providing diagrams to show some of the information; or
- organising the finished work ready for 'publishing'.

The differentiation by task would have to take account of what each child could offer so that all children make a realistic contribution to the joint outcome.

### Differentiation by resource

Allocating an LSA to work with a child is one example of differentiation by resource. Other examples could include:

- the provision of a laptop to address handwriting problems;
- providing children with a list of vocabulary or high-frequency words to reduce spelling barriers when children are composing a story;
- providing writing frames with more or less scaffolding, to take account of differing needs.

### Differentiation by content

If children are working on the same task, e.g. writing a story, playscript or report, differentiating the content by choice may help to motivate less able pupils. Children could be given the option to write their version as a horror story, adventure or fantasy. The task is the same for all pupils but allows for interest as the differentiating factor.

## Strategies for differentiating writing

Strategies for differentiating writing, and other tasks, occur most of the time, with teachers using a range of techniques in a coordinated way. Simply allowing a child more time to write something from the board, or to finish a piece on the computer is part of the natural technique of assembling all of the elements into a smooth, coordinated learning environment in which writing skills flourish.

## Accommodating the range of SEN

The range of SEN in any classroom affects its organisation. Each school has a unique mix of pupil population.

*The group with moderate learning difficulties*

Differentiating for the majority of this group may require little more than high expectations in addition to focused targets and approaches; complete access to literacy hour delivery; and reinforcement of writing across the wider curriculum.

*Pupils with challenging behaviour*

Disruptive behaviour can ruin superb lessons – instantly. Differentiation may require a plan B. If a child with behaviour problems is trying hard to conform, yet cannot get onto the computer when it is his turn because a child has not finished, he needs to know what to do. For example, in situations when the timing has gone wrong (as it does) could there be sets of jigsaw words or other short, independent activities which can be accessed without interrupting the teacher or other groups? If the child has an Individual Behaviour Plan (IBP), it may specify attention to task for a particular length of time, and differentiation by timing may well have to be a priority.



*The sensory impaired child*

How is an almost blind child to access a text for shared reading and to use a writing frame? Which writing group is best for a child with average ability yet with a hearing or visual impairment? For children with sensory impairments it is essential to consult the relevant Local Education Authority (LEA) service for advice or specialist equipment.

*The child with severe learning difficulties*

Children with severe learning difficulties require a range of differentiation strategies in order to benefit from literacy hour input. For example, the task of story writing may be adapted to picture writing, or a mixture of simple words with pictures in between to allow the child to compose. Do least able children write less, or are they allowed more time, according to their abilities and interest in the task?

*Children with specific learning difficulties*

As spelling is a major problem, differentiating composition could mean removing the spelling barrier and allowing pupils to shape their thoughts. Lists for high frequency spellings and subject vocabulary used in the right way can enable children with SpLD to use their imaginative strengths to the full, knowing that spelling work will feature elsewhere.

*The child with a severe handwriting difficulty*

Children with handwriting difficulties need time to produce a piece of extended writing. Differentiation may mean enhanced access to a computer so that the child can complete his text to coincide with completion time for the rest of the class.

Superb organisation cannot resolve every problem, but the issues raised should help teachers to identify the range of options from which to prioritise.

*Chapter 7*

# Writing – Methods and Approaches

How does the NLS benefit all learners? If the majority of children are to be 'held in' to the pace of teaching and learning, what kind of writing methods and approaches will address the needs of children with SEN?

## *The writing environment*

Positive teaching starts from the premise that all children can write given a facilitating writing environment. The points listed below merit consideration:

1. Class input should engage all learners at specific points throughout the lesson. Strategies for this could include:
   - personalising the content where appropriate, e.g. using children's names as models for the teaching point;
   - using children to 'help' with the presentation in some way, e.g. to turn pages; or
   - linking the objectives of the class lesson to specific writing targets where possible to engage less able pupils.

2. Teaching should build on children's strengths and eliminate weaknesses.

3. The short, sharp exchanges featured in the literacy hour help children with SEN to remain on task, if trained, whereas longer writing sessions do not 'hold in' struggling learners.

4. All children should perceive writing as a process. During shared writing sessions, alterations help children to see how process works to improve writing.

5. Choice aids motivation.

6. Boredom kills writing: if tasks start to become laborious, introduce a fresh sensory channel to the activity.

### Multi-sensory teaching and learning

What learners see, hear, touch, smell and taste contribute to the lasting strength of the learning experience. Applying this to spelling, a learner may:

- see the spelling patterns of the word;
- hear the rhythms of the word as he says it;
- feel the shapes of the letters within the word as he writes it; or
- use the meaning of the word and its relationships to help him remember it.

Multi-sensory activities use the eye, ear, hand and mind as communicating channels through which to coordinate learning experiences. A sequence from the NLS Module 3 video on sentence work illustrates a lesson based on punctuation, presented through the rhythm of music, with punctuation marks each represented by a particular instrument. The drum represented a full stop.

Children read the text together and heard the bang of the drum as they came to the end of a sentence. The child banging the drum would also feel the finality of the 'full stop' with each bang. Further examples may include:
- clapping syllables within words;
- saying words as they are written to aid spelling;
- children practising handwriting through the words they are learning to spell; and
- the human sentence technique, i.e. children stand in a line, each holding a word card and change places to show how word order affects the meaning of a sentence.

## Consistency and flexibility

Teachers' requirements vary. If children with SEN set out their writing one way, then have to set it out differently, they become confused. If pupils arrange their own work in accordance with agreed guidelines they develop sensible decision-making skills which enhance writing.

# *Teaching spelling and handwriting*

Multi-sensory approaches use spelling and handwriting to enrich each other. The 'look, say, cover, write and check' strategy uses four channels:
- *looking* helps learners to see the whole shape and supports the visual element;
- *saying* the word links it with language, so learners relate the spoken word with its written form;
- *covering* before writing the word ensures that it is written from memory and never copied;
- *checking* the written word makes learners look again (read it) and helps to commit the word to memory.

## Learning to spell

How is spelling acquired? Redfern (1993) reminds us that, 'at times, children use their eyes, and at others, their ears, to help them with spelling.' Module 2, Unit 3 of the NLS examines strategies for teaching children to spell irregular words. Strategies for teaching 'could' may include:
- placing it with its family – 'should' and 'would';
- using the onset and rime principle – 'ould' as the rime; or
- pointing out the phonic irregularity of this set of words and the need to memorise them graphically. But how would we then deal with 'mould'?

How do we teach 'what'? Options may include:
- emphasising its irregularity;
- placing it with its 'wh' family of question words – when, where, why, who, which;
- placing it with its vowel family – what, swat, squash.

Children with spelling difficulties need to understand why the strategy for spelling irregular words (using eyes) has to be different from spelling regular ones (using ears).

*Strategies/activities for developing spelling skills*

The following activities can help to develop spelling skills:
- talk with children about how words are made up;
- place words in families of letter patterns;
- teach children the method for learning spellings – look, say, cover, write, check – and explain why this is done;

- look at words with the same spellings and talk about their 'sameness';
- have pupils colour identical spelling features, or particular problems, e.g. the 'ai' in said;
- use tactile approaches, e.g. magnetic letters;
- have children insert missing letters in words, especially difficult vowel digraphs, unusual words or commonly mis-spelt words: th.y, s..d, th..r;
- finger-trace words in the air;
- write words on each other's backs (in pairs);
- pair a problem word to a known word, e.g. here and there;
- use mnemonics to help the learning process;
- colour small words inside larger ones — her, hero, there; or
- provide practice in seeing whole words from a mass of print, e.g. word search activities.

### *Use of nonsense words for spelling*

Non-words support learning in the following ways:

- spelling segmentation skills can be more accurately assessed in the secure knowledge that the 'word' being spelled cannot be a known one;
- practice in spelling 'fun' words (non-words) promotes confidence in all learners to try words they may not know the meaning of, for example in a dictation which may contain an unfamiliar word;
- spelling CVC non-words as well as words leads to the later strategy of spelling words with CVC beginnings and can help learners to find longer words in a dictionary — con, confidence, sen, sentence, dis, discussion, fam . . . ;
- interactive work with non-words places emphasis on segmentation skills without interfering with the main process of identifying component letters from what is heard;
- entering an 'unknown world' of words and letters promotes confidence in less able children to have a go; and
- the 'funny' spellings initiate much valuable discussion on the reasons for children's choices.

Children bring to a non-word activity what they know about real words. This provides opportunities to check their knowledge of letters, clusters and vowel digraphs and their strategies for attacking unknown spellings, and reveals their use of analogy to enter an unknown world of words.

The word 'unseachable' can be neither right nor wrong, but tells us a great deal about why the learner chose to spell what he heard in that particular way. The child's explanation could be, 'We've been working on syllables in class . . . so I knew about "un" and "able"' at the beginning and end of words. I thought it had three syllables, and the middle one rhymed with "peach" and "beach". It has the 'ea' in the middle because I always remember that "beach" goes with "sea". Used with care, non-words offer a valuable thinking strategy.

### *Rules for spelling*

As children reach the transitional stage, they can be helped to reduce errors by the use of rules, in addition to auditory and visual strategies. Spelling conventions and rules appear in the NLS Framework from Year 3. For example:

- how the spelling of verbs alter when -ing is added (Year 3, Term 1);
- how words change when -er, -est and -y are added (Year 3, Term 2);
- to . . . collect and classify spelling patterns in pluralisation . . . (Year 5, Term 1).

Rules build onto the visual and auditory skills children have acquired earlier, and support the transition towards 'correctness'. Rarely has learning a rule in isolation helped children to spell well.

*Proof-reading for spellings*

Help all children to become good proof-readers by:

- providing opportunities to read what is written;
- insisting that children check their own work;
- devising a consistent strategy for showing revised spellings, so that children know that neat crossings out are part of the redrafting and proof-reading process;
- teaching children how to work in pairs, to proof-read each other's writing in a sensitive way, with ground rules.

*Redrafting with the focus on spelling*

Redrafting with a single focus can work better for children with SEN. Searching only for spelling errors means that they:

- focus on the visual approach to spelling;
- keep spelling errors separate from distracting elements of writing which could be dealt with later;
- are not overwhelmed by a mass of text markings; and
- can link redrafting with their spelling targets, e.g. by having a checklist of high frequency words.

Children may need help to scan for spelling errors and may need a list of potential danger words e.g. 'their' and 'there', with attention drawn to the spelling within the sentence as part of the redrafting process.

*The magic line*

Spelling barriers block the creative process. The magic line enables writing flow to continue. Children put a line in place of a difficult word, with any letters the writer thinks are in it, and underlines it for checking later, which helps children to write without worrying about difficult spelling. At the end of the initial session, response partner work can address the spelling issues. Pairs of children can then share dictionary skills to find the words they need.

*Safe spellers*

Safe spellers have become prisoners of their own spelling limitations and lack confidence to attempt new words. They search for words they know rather than take risks. To encourage safe spellers to break out:

- encourage and reward the use of alternative words;
- provide oral language activities to build up vocabulary and let children visualise new words;
- discuss synonyms and antonyms;
- praise attempts at spelling new words, however incorrect;
- point out the correct letters in the word;
- provide spelling games which encourage risk-taking;
- extend reading, with discussion of new vocabulary; and
- involve safe spellers in interactive text construction.

## The 'try it first' book

Children who have been given spellings cannot learn spelling strategies. An exercise book can be used for children to try first, before asking. The record helps children to see improvements in their attempts as they go along.

*A learn-to-spell wordbook*

Learning to spell the high frequency words listed in the NLS Framework, or core subject vocabulary, is easier if a wordbook is used. Spellings for the half-term can be listed at the front, and those to be learned each week can be identified by a colour. Those for week 1 may be in blue, week 2 in yellow, and so on, and each week the child learns set spellings using the strategies taught.

Pupils of similar ability could test each other using a dated page of the wordbook. The learn-to-spell wordbook provides evidence for assessment and helps to keep track of what is being learned as part of any long-term spelling plan. It also helps to inform the pupil's IEP review meeting, and is a useful way of including incorrectly spelt core subject vocabulary. The pupil lists in a specified part of the wordbook a number of words from the week, according to ability. The 'my own words' strategy helps children to take responsibility for their own spellings and helps them to transfer spelling work to other areas of the curriculum.

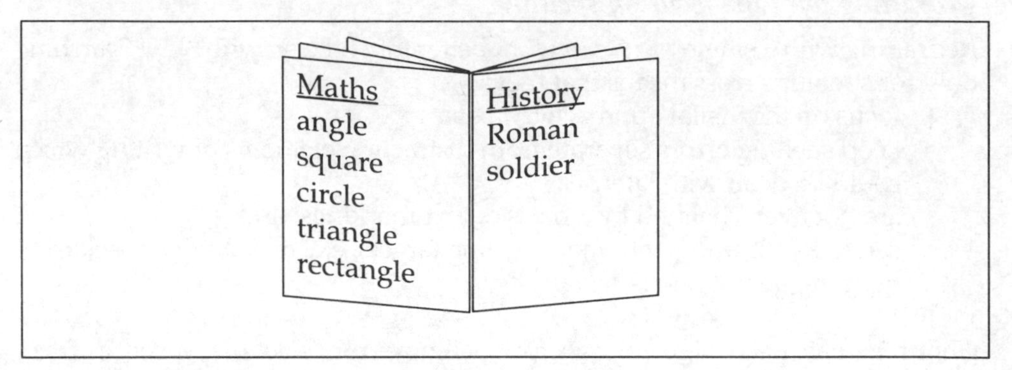


**Figure 7.1** Wordbook for cross-curricular vocabulary

*Pupils with SpLD*

The Bullock Report *A Language for Life* states, 'It has to be accepted that some people will have difficulty with spelling all their lives, but we believe that the teacher can bring about substantial improvement with the majority of children' (Bullock 1975; 11.42.). SpLD is often equated with dyslexia and, as difficulties with spelling affect all dyslexics, ways to minimise the problems need to be sought.

Attwood (1994) stated that assessment poses acute problems for dyslexic pupils. The following questions are adapted from the areas of difficulty identified:

- how far should dyslexic children take part in standardised tests which are not part of their spelling programme?
- should dyslexic children be given extra time to learn spellings before being tested on particular words?
- should marking identify every spelling mistake?
- should spelling work from focused spelling lessons, or in the literacy hour, be marked differently from writing in other areas of the curriculum?
- should the spelling of identified dyslexic children be assessed differently to that of other pupils?

Any significant and persistent difficulty in reading, sentence structure and spelling, in comparison with observed abilities in other areas of learning, needs to be thoroughly investigated by a relevant specialist. As these difficulties are likely to form a barrier to written work it is essential that they are identified and addressed through an IEP which states precisely what is to be done, by whom, and how.

## Thrass for spelling and handwriting

Thrass supports the teaching of handwriting, reading and spelling skills in an integrated way. The backbone of the system is the Thrass chart of the 44 phonemes represented by the 26 letters of the English alphabet. The chart offers a choice of graphemes for each phoneme. For example, if the child tries to spell 'breeze', the 'z' sound could be represented by any one of five possible sounds for 'z' which appear on the Thrass chart – zip, fizz, sneeze, laser or cheese. The grapheme selection, assisted by analogy, e.g. breeze sounds more like sneeze or cheese than any of the other choices, appears to work in developing spelling skills for all children, but particularly for those with SEN.

Spelling forms a major area of writing difficulty for many children and causes misery for the few learners with SpLD. When spelling an unknown word children may revert to previous stages: one piece of writing can reveal several stages of spelling development. Spelling gets the better of many of us. Which of the spellings below are wrong?

| | | | | | |
|---|---|---|---|---|---|
| liquify | desicate | sieze | weird | broccoli | assassin |
| atlasses | focusing | vermilion | parrafin | inoculate | |

## Developing handwriting and preventing problems

A sensitive and consistent handwriting policy minimises future problems. This section and the following eight points highlight SEN concerns.

1. Nothing is more important than correct letter formation. It is the child's introduction to handwriting and its first problem area, and bad habits learned at this stage tend to stick. A few key points:
   - watch children form their letters, to ensure they are the right way round;
   - whole-school consistency of policy is crucial;
   - use tactile, multi-sensory approaches, e.g. a bag with letters inside for children to identify by touch;
   - emphasise the main significant features of each letter, e.g. the cross on the 't', or the dot on the 'i';
   - talk about the similarities and differences between letters to help children sort them out in their minds;
   - letter formation should always be linked to the sound of the letter and its name;
   - link letters with words and use children's names as much as possible;
   - give them some reminders and good rules to remember, e.g. all letters except 'd' and 'e' start at the top;
   - keep practice sessions short to retain interest;
   - praise handwriting which shows good significant features, e.g. ascenders and descenders, space between words.

   Should letters be joined or not joined from the beginning? What is the relationship of pattern practice to letter formation? Jarman (1979) suggests that, 'a completely joined hand is not recommended as a first introduction to writing as . . . children need to understand the separate nature of the letters.' On the other hand, 'joined patterns are recommended because flow, regularity, and consistency are inherent in them'. The NLS Framework suggests three objectives for reception children: a comfortable and efficient pencil grip; a controlled line which supports letter formation; and correct sequence of movements.

   From Year 1, Term 1, the NLS objectives include:
   - to form lower case letters in a script that will be easy to join later.

   From Year 1, Term 2, links with spelling are mentioned:
   - to practise handwriting in conjunction with spelling and independent writing.

   From Year 2, Term 1, the use of 'the four basic handwriting joins' start to feature, and by Year 2, Term 3, handwriting practises phonic and spelling

patterns from word level work.
At various stages, it is worth explaining to learners why they are practising patterns or letters with flicks ready for joining. To aid letter formation, words containing particular letters can be displayed with the focus letter highlighted, to help children to see each letter in context, i.e. as part of a word. Children with learning difficulties may be seeing letters as insignificant shapes.

2. Clarity and consistency of lettering. It is confusing to see many variations of the same letter from the early stages of learning to form them. Does the 't' have a curve or not? At some point, children need to meet variations in font, but by then they should be able to recognise the main features of each letter to identify it.

3. Children with handwriting difficulties struggle to produce speed and neatness at the same time. From Year 4, the NLS objectives suggest that children should know when to use:
   - a clear, neat hand for finished, presented work;
   - informal writing for every day . . . rough drafting, etc.

   If speed is a main feature when getting information from the board or worksheet, then children need to know this. If neatness is a main feature when presenting a final draft for an audience, they need time to produce it. Maintaining balance will help children to produce what is wanted without anxiety.

4. During handwriting practice, learners should be able to understand what they write. If the letter groups and words have no meaning, the multi-sensory approach is lost, and children are merely writing patterns.

5. Where handwriting practice links spellings being learned, the activity benefits both. The same principle applies to phonics. Meaningful links between letter clusters and handwriting sessions will benefit both sets of skills.

6. Children's attitudes to handwriting are essential to their learning – letters have to be correctly formed for cursive writing to be achieved. But when personal style takes over, does it matter about the loop on the 'l' or the way in which descenders are formed? Rigidity long after it has ceased to matter has turned many children with SEN off cursive writing.

7. How far does 'best' handwriting have to appear in every lesson and for what purpose? There are many facets to this problem. The first is that many children with SEN only see handwriting as part of English lessons. They need to be shown that writing in history, science and other subjects may require writing at presentation standard some of the time.
   Many children are unsure when handwriting matters and when other factors of writing (e.g. speed) matter more. The author has observed children making notes in their best handwriting, and not completing the task, because they thought they had to 'write in their best' at all times. Less able children need to be shown how handwriting features in the movement of tasks between process and the final product.

8. A choice of tools can help less able children to retain interest and develop learning. Redfern and Walker (1994) suggest that, 'soft pencils and pens with fibre tips are easier to use than ballpoint pens'. If variety is available, children can be helped to choose suitable tools for the job.

*Handwriting difficulties and the dyspraxic child*

Dr Rosemary Sassoon (1991) reminds us of the need to understand handwriting in order to deal with problems. Sassoon states that, 'When teaching, it is the hand that needs to be trained in the intricate movements that produce letters. Hand and eye need to work together . . . As dyspraxic children may have a combination of problems involving coordination, sequencing or organising themselves, these will be mirrored in their writing.' Poor handwriting is seldom the writer's fault but it indicates a difficulty. If, in spite of consistent teaching, a child is experiencing severe and persistent handwriting problems, it is important to seek the advice of a specialist.

## *Linking word, sentence and text level*

The NLS Framework identifies objectives at word, sentence and text level which, in practice, are integrated together in writing activities. Vocabulary extension work appears in the word level column, but its place in the sentence determines the most appropriate choice of word. Text type and genre also help to influence the words used. When making notes, and later reassembling notes for project work, where does word, sentence and text level work begin and end?

### From sentence to text

Many children struggle to compose a sequence of sentences, failing to see how each sentence stems from the last. The author has found the following approach successful with many less able children. The strategy follows a series of steps:

1. During shared writing sessions initiate, for step 1, a number of sentences (one for each group) which stimulate some depth of thought, for example:
   - there are too many cars on the roads; or
   - school holidays should be spread out.

   Make sure children avoid 'dead end' sentences which go nowhere, such as, 'the sky is blue'. The sentences are written on strips of card for each group to take one as their task.

2. Each group composes three or four more sentences about the whole of their opening sentence, not a part of it, using a particular colour of card (label it 'step 2').

3. Again, using coloured card labelled 'step 3', sentences are jointly initiated from each of the ones at step 2, generating at least ten sentences from the original as illustrated in Figure 7.2. The collection of sentences from each group form a good talking point for a plenary session.

**Making sentences**

| Step 1 | Step 2 | Step 3 |
|---|---|---|
| There are too many cars on the roads | It's not healthy | Fumes are bad for you. They mak asma wurs. They pollut the air. |
| | Old people cant get acros. | They will get nocked down. They cant run. |
| | We get trafick jams. | Drivers get fed up. They shout at each other. We arelait for school. |

**Figure 7.2** From sentence to text

4. Step 4 could follow a similar pattern, the aim being to go into further detail about what has been already generated.

This kind of task can spill over into two or three writing sessions, and use cross-curricular content. Less able writers can contribute at their own level.

### Directed activities with texts

Activities which develop reading comprehension also support writing composition. Activities for sequencing could include:

- writing sentences on cards and jigsaw cutting into phrases for other groups to match up;
- sequencing mixed up sentences into paragraphs to help them to write paragraphs as one main idea;
- older children could write multi-clause sentences onto card, and cut up for other groups to fit together; and
- at later stages, paragraphs from newspapers and magazines could be matched up into sections.

Encourage detailed writing by:

- using question words – who, what, how, when, where, and particularly why;
- develop descriptive language – people, places, situations;
- at sentence level, looking at the functions of verbs, adverbs, nouns and adjectives; and
- getting pupils to think in pictures and describe in words.

Activities which focus on the main idea could include:

- group writing of an opening paragraph;
- writing the first sentence of a paragraph as the main idea, with other sentences to support it;
- 'spider webbing' a topic to show chapters, sections and paragraphs each as sub-sets of main ideas; or
- experimenting with different titles and talking about which is most effective and why.

Develop pupils' understanding of cause and effect by:

- composing first halves of sentences which use 'because', i.e. 'The tree was blown over because . . .'
- talking about and using phrases which focus on cause and effect at text level – 'because of this . . .', 'in spite of . . .' ; or
- emphasising the function of 'why'.

Focus on making comparisons by:

- talking about and using comparative phrases;
- writing about comparative or opposite events and situations, e.g. a stormy sky and a calm, sunny sky;
- comparing different people, careers, countries, holidays – for example, a ski holiday and a beach holiday; or
- writing to compare different genres or authors from the fiction texts read during the year.

Text types from the environment help the modelling process: compare newspapers, comics, leaflets, notices or holiday brochures, as well as plays, novels and poetry.

## Working at deeper text levels

Activities requiring pupils to reorganise text develop their manipulation of written language. These could include:

- changing tenses – from past to present, to future;
- changing person – from first to third, or to second;
- changing viewpoint in a piece of fiction; or
- asking pupils to represent information in diagrammatic form – Venn diagrams, charts, matrices etc.

A high level of thinking takes place when pupils reorganise text or present data by means of a diagram. Such activities move all pupils' writing forward. Directed writing tasks with texts should take place through class or group activities, using shared reading or writing as the stimulus. Children with SEN learn from such activities provided that language is properly understood.

## Teaching grammar through atmosphere and emotion

The use of exciting texts as the stimulus for grammar work stands a better chance of reaching less able writers. The starting point with fiction could be how writers create atmospheric tension, or emotion, by specific techniques. During shared and guided writing, analyse the techniques used by authors to create special effects – pupils often fail to realise that grammar, choice of vocabulary and punctuation have a specific function. Below are a few suggestions for discussion topics:

1. Why are sentences short? What effect is created? Children could write dramatic sentences, using three, two or single words to create effect – Wow!

2. How do authors balance long and short sentences, and why? Talk about the rhythm of language.

3. Verbs and nouns should create their own impact in the text – ran quickly, sprinted, walked slowly, strolled. Children could play around with words to create different effects.

4. For punctuation:
   - take it out of the text, have groups of pupils put it in, then talk about and compare each group's version;
   - analyse the function of different punctuation, using different text types – full stop, comma, dashes and dots.

## Working with poetry

Poetry is exciting, yet many pupils fail to see the point of it. Poetry must represent pleasure if less able children are going to attempt to write it. When teaching poetry:

- free forms of poetry are easier for less able children with restricted language;
- teach children that a good poem will end each line with a strong word, rather than a bland one;
- teach children that lines of poetry are not sentences;
- avoid reading poems that are too obscure;
- use pictures and objects to stimulate colourful phrases;
- talk about techniques used in poetry to create effects;
- clap out rhythms of poems;
- try not to let spelling and handwriting problems stifle the creative process;
- include shape poems for fun;

- create interest in poetry through short, sharp bursts; for example, read a short poem before playtime, display a poem of the week, focus on a particular poet, add music to poems or tape poems.

If reluctant writers can be stimulated to write poetry, it may inspire them to write other text types, simply because of poetry's brevity and its lack of reliance on sentence structures and paragraphs. Poetry still requires technique, but may be less daunting than a complete story or a class book.

### Note-making skills

For many children, copying from texts is preferable to taking and making notes. Malone and Smith (1996) comment that, 'unless the learner can write swiftly and legibly and can spell automatically, note-taking will serve little purpose'.

On the other hand, leaving aside dictated notes, learners need to be able to make notes from reference texts in the library and build them up into prose for project work. Note-making is a joint reading and writing activity involving comprehension, selection, and restructuring.

The NLS Framework for writing composition in Year 5, Term 1 requires pupils to:

- make notes for different purposes;
- use simple abbreviations in note-taking.

For less able children the following strategies may help:

- demonstrate good and poor examples of notes;
- talk in groups or as a class about the purpose of notes;
- teach pupils that good notes include meaning-carrying words and discard function words (in, on, the);
- ask groups to make different notes from texts for other groups to build into prose;
- ask pupils to highlight function words (and, is, when, that) in a light colour, and main meaning-carrying phrases in a brighter colour to make them 'jump out' from the text.

## *Removing anxiety – building confidence*

Many children lack the ability to control a story or a longer piece of non-fiction writing and will benefit from group activities which remove some of their anxiety. Through group writing, all children can:

- understand the structure of fiction and non-fiction;
- share tasks of editing and revision;
- discuss vocabulary choices, sentences, paragraphs; or
- be helped with spelling and presentation.

While group writing benefits less able writers, it must build up their confidence to do some writing alone. How else are learners to develop, and how can teachers observe individual skills and strategies to guide children forward?

Alston (1995) comments that less able pupils write less than their classmates and cumulatively lose a great deal of practice time for writing. She states that, 'By the junior years the habit of not knowing what to write and of writing little has usually become well established'. Group approaches reduce anxiety and promote confidence, enabling less able pupils to write more. All pupils benefit from integrated word, sentence and text level activities with a clear focus to the objectives and a sensitive understanding of children's writing needs. Effective methods and approaches rely partly on the right resources to back them up, and these resources will be discussed in the next chapter.

*Chapter 8*

# Resources for Writing

As any writer will tell you, nothing is worse than staring at a blank page. While resources for reading invite much discussion in schools, those for writing may be seen as less of a priority, yet the pen and paper may need to be supported by a more interesting variety of equipment.

The following sections outline key issues for choosing writing resources, and ideas for using equipment and games. Resources for writing, purchased or home-made, need to be:

- suitable for their purpose, i.e. NLS teaching objective;
- age-appropriate for learners to use;
- relevant to what different groups of learners need;
- interesting;
- accessible for all children using them;
- multi-sensory where possible;
- able to be used for a variety of activities; and
- non-consumable where possible.

## *Basic writing needs*

The following sections offer suggestions for gathering together basic tools for shared and guided writing.

### Models of text types

First on the list must be samples of the range of text types for modelling, which need to balance fiction and non-fiction.

*Fiction*

The fiction collection needs to include stories, plays and poetry. Teachers should question whether:

- the range of fiction represents every cultural need;
- different interests are provided for;
- materials stretch to the age range (a mixed age class);
- plays have differentiated parts;
- poems for modelling illustrate different forms – haiku, sonnets and narrative poems as well as free form;
- there are sensitive topics to be dealt with carefully;
- there are enough fiction models to stimulate boys;
- the range includes different kinds of books, e.g. pop-up books, to inspire class book-making; and
- traditional as well as modern texts are included.

*Non-fiction*

Non-fiction needs to account for 50 per cent of the writing done in school and must include the range of text types which have been identified by their function: recount, report, procedure, explanation, persuasion, discussion/argument. The functions identified represent the main types of non-fiction.

This range could also include different models of each text type, e.g. texts for persuasion may include examples of advertisements as well as persuasive prose. Models for non-fiction need not be costly: pupils enjoy bringing leaflets, adverts, lists, notices, brochures and so on for the school collection.

### Writing frames

Writing frames are a key part of shared and guided writing, and need to be chosen carefully. Schools may ask the following questions:

- will the writing frame achieve its purpose for all learners?
- are the 'starter phrases' suitable for children who are to use them, without sounding unnatural?
- does the frame allow the right amount of scaffolding without stifling children's creativity?
- can all children read the scaffolding phrases on the frame or do less able children need an adapted version?
- are children with English as a second language provided for by the writing frame?

Writing frames are effective tools for teaching writing but need to be accessed by all learners if they are to help raise writing standards. Lewis and Wray (1996) point out that, 'Writing in a range of genres is most effective if it is located in meaningful experiences . . . frames should always be used as part of class topic work rather than in isolated study skill lessons.' The authors also comment that the frames themselves offer no purpose for writing.

### Various implements for writing

As well as pens and pencils, does the store of writing implements include markers, highlighters, fibre tips and other colourful writing tools? Are there special holders for young writers to help train the correct grip?

### Assorted writing paper

If children can sometimes use different colours, weights and textures of paper, it may encourage more pupils to write at length. The exercise book may need to be the main writing material, yet other materials may prove more cost-effective in pupil motivation if the final draft could sometimes be presented on an alternative. A variety of colour and texture enhances wall display and provides the stimulus for meaningful discussion of print and background choices.

### Assorted card

If pupils are to work in pairs and larger groups and to take part in interactive activities and games, coloured card works better than paper. Generating dialogue in groups can use colour to record who has said what. If the work is displayed on the writing wall, coloured card enhances access for less able pupils. Have sentence-length card ready-cut for a smooth start to group work. Word size pieces enable instant access when groups are to work on spelling and word level games, and the fluorescent cards used by shopkeepers to display prices are also useful, as colour enhances aspects of learning. For example for multi-clause sentence work, the use of colour helps pupils to see the main and subordinate elements of the sentence.

### Assorted pictures

Pictures have always provided a stimulus for writing. The aim is for children to use pictures effectively as an aid to writing. A few suggestions to aid this are as follows:

- for young or less able writers, avoid a picture with too much clutter. If children are to write a story or a poem from class discussion, the picture stimulus should not detract from the clear focus of the writing;
- try using black and white pictures as a change from colour;
- group pictures according to mood, or the way in which they lend themselves to different writing, e.g. description, character traits;
- pictures help children to focus. Many fiction writers have pictures of people, from magazines etc. which epitomise their characters. Children too may create more rounded characters in their story with pictures to help; and
- include pictures of football, sports etc. to interest boys.

However focused the writing, as pupils finish early, the last thing a teacher wants is children with nothing to do. Pictures from old catalogues and magazines may inspire them to write short pieces from choice, which could develop as extended pieces.

## *Resources for spelling*

Spelling resources are likely to include the following items:

1. A selection of letters, which may be plastic, wooden, magnetic or interlocking (which do not move as the child carries his formed word out to the front).

2. Spelling workbooks – these cannot teach children how to spell. Their purpose is to provide practice on the teaching points which have featured during interactive work. The problem with spelling workbooks is the tendency for children to plough through page after page, thinking the aim is to get to the end, then onto the next book (rather like their attitude to reading schemes). For workbooks to be effective, the words must have been worked on orally to ensure all children know what they mean. Teachers should ask:
   - is the workbook clear and not cluttered for the less able?
   - can children work on them independently following the interactive preparatory work?
   - do the workbooks link spelling with handwriting?
   - do the workbooks reflect the policy of the school on spelling and handwriting?
   - do the workbooks reflect stilted sentence structures which could place a negative influence on children's developing use of sentence writing, i.e. too much use of 'Here is John' or 'The pan is black'?

For all children, and for manageability, workbooks play some part in written work. For children with SEN, two sources of materials have been found useful and accessible:

- Easylearn (see useful addresses) provide a range of workbook materials, including punctuation for use in Key Stage 2; and
- Learning Materials Ltd (see useful addresses) produce workbooks for the range of writing, many of which come with cassettes.

### Additional spelling resources

Many pupils with SEN have benefited from the following:

1. The PAT programme (Phonological Awareness Training) has been found useful with all groups. A beginners book includes worksheets, records, spelling lists and phrases for dictation work which can all be photocopied. This is followed by similar materials for Level 1, Level 2 and Level 3 for

syllables (see useful addresses). Each PAT session requires only 10 to 15 minutes.

2. H.E.L.P. - help eliminate learning problems – games are fun to use, designed for children with SEN, but can be enjoyed by all. The games focus on phonic work as combined skills for reading and spelling.

3. Thrass is gaining popularity as a resource for teaching handwriting, reading and spelling as a combined approach. Thrass is most effective as a whole school resource where consistency of teaching approach is the main feature.

4. Word searches and crosswords: these are not only fun to use, but encourage children to see whole words from a mass of print. Word searches are quick to make, using ready squared sheets, and develop children's reading and spelling of irregular words. Crosswords focus on spelling and meaning together, and help to develop spelling skills by making the learner think about the most likely letters for the available space.

5. Special Needs Learning Materials (see useful addresses) produce a number of ideas for games, with hints for differentiation, e.g. shape spelling which helps children to remember words.

6. Stile materials enable pupils to self-check and are useful for independent activities. Stile spelling is available as part of a range of literacy packages from LDA/NES Arnold (see useful addresses).

### Purchased kits for combined phonic work

Resource kits for teaching phonological awareness and/or phonic skills have mushroomed since the NLS emphasis on phonics. Resource kits such as Jolly Phonics, Letterland and Rhyme World (see useful addresses) are three the author has found useful. A phonic resource kit can be a valuable addition to the Key Stage 1 classroom as it provides a consistent structure to teaching phonics, and a range of multi-sensory resources.

Phonic resource kits are intended for Key Stage 1 children and may be inappropriate for older pupils who have fallen behind. Other users of Letterland and Jolly Phonics have commented on how children enjoy the fun activities. With Letterland, the focus on characters and stories as the medium for learning phonics is a strong point. However, older children need to be weaned off such resources as soon as it is appropriate. Less able pupils have been known to cling to the character references, e.g. 'hill' and 'hot' begin with 'hairy hat man', well into Key Stage 2, which does not support growing maturity.

## *Resources for handwriting*

The most important resource for handwriting is that of a consistent approach by every teacher in the school. Resources for handwriting need to link with those for spelling as far as possible. Handwriting booklets which contain practice exercises should enable children to read what they write, and handwriting resources need to include equipment which reinforces letter formation, e.g. a rollerball. Seeing where the letter starts and the movement of the ball is an essential prerequisite to worksheet practice for less able children.

## *Resources for sentence and text work*

There are many published materials for sentence and text work in the literacy hour, some of which can be purchased as sets with different elements. For example, a school may purchase a literacy set containing plays; comprehension cards; sentence making blocks and a variety of card games for reading and spelling.

Such resources are intended for short, sharp activity sessions rather than longer time spans. Many resources, such as sentence-making bricks, may work best with children in pairs rather than larger groups. While such resources are useful, their success lies in the way in which pupils are organised to work with them. As with many resources, it is tempting to fit children around what is available, rather than match the resource to the literacy needs of particular groups.

## *Reference materials*

Independence in reading and writing depends on the reference section, which may contain a selection of dictionaries and alphabet friezes; thesauruses; atlases; tip cards of useful information for spelling; and encyclopaedias.

### Choosing dictionaries

Dictionaries come in all shapes and sizes depending on their purpose, and all children should be shown how to access the right one at each learning stage. It is easier for children with learning difficulties to ask rather than use a dictionary, especially if the process is arduous and time consuming. When choosing a dictionary schools may question: which children are to use it? Can they access it? What kinds of dictionary resources are needed from the range available: a first alphabet type dictionary; picture dictionaries; illustrated dictionaries; thematic dictionaries; key word dictionaries (subject related words), or ACE spelling dictionaries (where pupils need only to know how words sound in order to spell them).

Dictionaries should be age-appropriate, since nothing is more embarrassing for an older child than to be given a picture dictionary. Children with SEN may need support in using a dictionary for its range of purposes, for checking spellings, for looking up meanings and to check word forms for sentence work. All children need to regard dictionaries as user-friendly resources for literacy independence: from Year 1, Term 2, the NLS objective is to 'use simple dictionaries and to understand their alphabetical organisation'.

### Using a thesaurus

From Reception year, vocabulary extension plays a key role in literacy as children start to 'make collections of personal interest or significant words linked to particular topics' as suggested in the NLS Framework. By Year 2, children should be, 'discussing similarities and shades of meaning . . . to extend and enhance writing', and from Year 3 they are to, 'understand the purpose and organisation of the thesaurus and to make use of it to find synonyms'. The thesaurus has traditionally been less used as a resource than the dictionary, yet it is a valuable vocabulary aid.

### Tip cards of useful information

Independence can be enhanced by having useful information handy. The Basic Skills Agency (see useful addresses) produce tip cards for days of the week, number words, etc. which may motivate less able children to strive for independence.

### Encyclopaedias

A range of skills is required to access encyclopaedias: children need to know how the information is shared between each volume, before they can find what they want and make notes. For children with an insecure knowledge of the alphabet, a chart above the reference area could indicate the chunk of alphabet assigned to each volume. Single volume encyclopaedias act as a stepping stone for less able pupils.

## Writing with the OHP

Creative use of the OHP can make a simple resource go a long way. The OHP can help pupils' motivation, especially if they can use it as well, and OHP acetates can be used many times if they are laminated first. The OHP could be an exciting way to generate shared writing.

## ICT resourcing

The use of the computer as a tool and an aid to motivation should not overshadow the literacy objectives. Useful resources (see useful addresses) include:

- GAMZ – 'swap and fix' are produced in a choice of 28 card games, plus a CD-ROM, and a separately available word search generator for Windows with cross-curricular use;
- 'Word Shark' published by White Space is a phonic resource for teaching reading and spelling in a fun way, and is targeted to assist children with SpLD;
- 'Units of Sound' is a multimedia program, again targeted mainly at children with SpLD but, as with most multi-sensory resources, useful for all learners;
- The Early Learning and Special Needs Educational Software catalogue contains a wealth of software to support writing, much of which extends across the curriculum. Included among a range of programs for writing are:
  - 'My First Incredible Amazing Dictionary', which claims to talk, teach and to entertain its users;
  - 'Talking Textease' and 'Talking Write Away' which both have spell-checkers which can point out errors in what the child has typed in. Textease is a super program for simple desk-top publishing and will help pupils to plan and draft their writing in a fun oriented way;
  - 'Startwrite' is designed to help poor spellers;
  - 'Co:Writer' is designed to help children who struggle with physical disabilities, dyslexia and other learning difficulties. This works with any word processor to make writing faster and easier.

Computer software only supports learning if it does what is required and can be accessed independently. If the software is to develop reading and writing, the teaching objectives must guide the selection and, as with any software, it is more cost-effective to have a few selected programs which are used often than to have many which are only used now and again.

## Resources for home and school use

Given the thrust towards parental partnership, resources which link home and school could be useful. Children with learning difficulties, or those who have few literacy materials to work on at home, could be inspired through the 'home-work resources' available from publishers (e.g. Folens; see useful addresses).

## Other ideas from teachers

Some staff have suggested using individual whiteboards for written work as an alternative when the work does not have to be kept as a record. Alternatively, sheets of paper can be laminated for repeated use with marker pens and wiped clean. However, no resources can take the place of interactive work with a skilled adult, or with peers.

*Chapter 9*

# Writing Across the Curriculum

## *The role of writing across the curriculum*

There are sound reasons why all children need to reinforce writing skills across subject areas. For example:

- all writing needs cannot fit into the literacy hour;
- subject writing offers a range of contexts for practice;
- subject writing contributes to evidence for assessment; and
- pupils are more likely to view writing as a learning aid.

Booklets published by the Qualifications and Curriculum Authority (QCA) in 1997, entitled *Use of Language – A Common Approach* stress the contribution of all subjects to writing practice and communication.

## *Writing in subject areas*

The range of writing done in subject areas may include the following:

- copying information from a board or worksheet;
- finding information and making notes from reference texts;
- organising information to present to the class or groups;
- writing which reflects on learning, such as a log or journal;
- writing as part of pupils' own assessment and recording;
- writing in diagrammatic format, e.g. assembling information into a Venn diagram, bar chart or graph;
- class or group brainstorming activities for writing;
- writing which reorganises subject-based text in various ways, e.g. by writing a historical event as a play; or
- writing which records group thinking about a subject topic, e.g. opposing views of a group debate.

The list illustrates the potential of subject writing for encouraging learners to practise their writing skills and inject sensible decision-making into their composition.

## *Writing and English*

The NLS does not replace English in the National Curriculum. NLS objectives provide a detailed structure behind the programmes of study for reading and writing. Objectives for listening and speaking are not included within the structure of the NLS, but are its foundation, while reading and writing develop through focused and interactive talk.

Drama should still feature as a medium for extending written work, e.g. playscripts generated in the literacy hour. Drama can play a key role in deepening pupils' understanding of subject content and vocabulary.

The general requirements for English suggest that pupils, 'read, analyse and evaluate a wide range of . . . literature from the English literary heritage (and) other cultures and traditions.' (p2, English in the National Curriculum; DfE 1995.) The study of literature is a study of writing.

## *Writing to learn*

Two questions must be answered here:

- how is literacy reinforced through subject learning?
- how can teachers integrate learning to write with writing to learn?

Literacy links with the subject curriculum should not be contrived, yet if the NLS is to work for all pupils, opportunities for natural links need to be fully exploited.

### Using frames to support subject writing

While scaffolding writing through frames has many benefits, Rees (1996) points out that, 'children should read, discuss and write different types of text because of the communicative purposes they want to achieve, not because they are working through a checklist of written varieties.' Using frames for subject writing is a positive strategy, and will help less able pupils with shape and form, yet all children need the freedom to think and make decisions. The point of scaffolding is to support, but not to imprison, writing creativity.

### Using subject dictionaries

Many children with learning difficulties struggle to be independent with subject writing because the spelling of core vocabulary blocks the writing process. When a child has agonised over the same spelling, or struggled to write a sentence because concepts are unclear, inspiration fades. A subject dictionary with words and meanings, or possibly with pictures, can help all children to be independent. Figure 9.1 illustrates a simple version for work on medieval life.

| **Subject dictionary — Medieval life** | |
|---|---|
| **Word** | **Meaning** |
| abbott's house | where the head monk lives |
| almonry | where monks give food to the poor |
| archery | shooting with a bow and arrows |
| armour | metal to protect the body, e.g. chain mail |

**Figure 9.1** Using a subject dictionary

Key word dictionaries (e.g. Folens) work on the principle of grouping words together into topics for easy reference, with pictures. Training children with SEN to access subject and key word dictionaries enables them to work independently in the literacy hour and in subject writing time.

### Using vocabulary lists, cue cards and picture cards

Placing vocabulary lists inside the cover of exercise books helps to minimise pupils' dependence upon an adult or peer for spellings. Provided vocabulary has been discussed and comprehension has been checked out, vocabulary lists support less able writers. The words placed in the exercise book for reference may also be the same subject words identified for all children to learn to spell. As they become known, words can be removed from the reference list and others added.

Cue cards with a word and picture on help pupils to recall vocabulary they have forgotten. During the writing process, if they need a reminder of what words mean, they look at the cue cards filed in the reference area. Pupils themselves or SEN support assistants could make cue cards from a list of core vocabulary for each subject during the forthcoming term: such activities also utilise pupil energy during wet playtimes. The same cards could be used for subject games and other work.

## Matching text types to subject writing

Teachers could identify the range of text types generated from one topic. For example, a study of the Romans might include writing:

- a recount of a visit to the Roman museum;
- a letter from a soldier based in Britain to his family in Rome (a recount of his experiences);
- a notice to advertise the next chariot race (persuasion);
- a notice advertising training for would-be gladiators (persuading them to join up);
- menus for a Roman banquet from having read about what the Romans ate;
- a book of recipes for Roman cooks (procedure);
- a contract for a slave;
- a speech to be delivered to the Roman Senate; or
- a discussion paper reflecting on various aspects of the Romans, inviting group or class debate (argument) on topics such as 'Why were the Romans a civilisation?' or 'What were the main causes of their decline?'

Alternatively, one text type could be tracked across the different subjects. For this purpose we might consider the attributes of procedural writing. Writing a procedure usually involves a statement of what is to be achieved, and has a sequence of stages. Examples could include writing:

- the rules for a new maths game;
- recipes for groups to try in food technology;
- instructions for safely getting out the PE equipment;
- instructions for setting up a new computer; or
- procedural instructions for mixing paint in art.

If children have achieved a pleasing effect, e.g. of a stormy sky, a group of trees, or still life, they could write up their technique for other groups, stating which colours were used and how the effect is achieved. Such writing will be seen by pupils as real, shared and purposeful.

Cross-curricular explanation texts may involve writing:

- to explain a mathematical point – why two quarters are the same as one half (and demonstrate maths knowledge);
- how a model constructed in technology lessons works;
- how the rain cycle works;
- how the Aborigines find water in the Australian desert;
- why we should eat lots of fruit and vegetables;
- why volcanoes erupt; or
- why the Industrial Revolution is so called.

Explanations often focus on the how and why of natural happenings, or social events, and usually state reasons as causes and effects.

Finally, we might consider persuasive writing across the curriculum. This could include writing:

- a statement of viewpoint for group discussion, e.g. I think our school uniform colours should be red and navy. My reasons are – red is a bright colour for a jumper; navy will not show marks as quickly; red and navy go together well.
- adverts – for selling home-made cakes at the school fair;
- for a book swap (e.g. why is this book good?).

Pieces of writing often involve more than one text type. For example, a report may include explanation, and persuasive writing can include balanced alternative points which make it an argument or item for discussion. Categories for text types are guides to thinking about the many different kinds of non-fiction writing across the curriculum.

## Diagrammatic formats

Figure 9.2 illustrates diagrammatic formats from subject work. Many children struggle to understand data presented as diagrams, and struggle even more to construct them. If all children are taught to organise information using different formats, it will enhance reading, writing and subject knowledge.

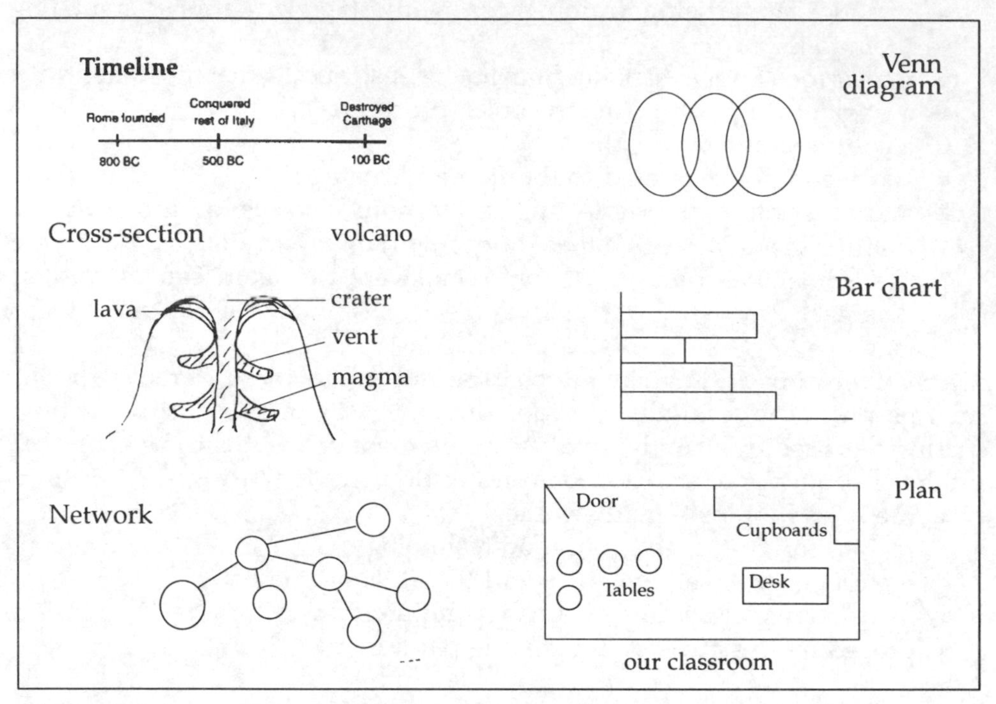


**Figure 9.2** Constructing diagrammatic format

What is the function of each diagram? How does a flow chart represent procedural information? Why is a matrix or a bar chart better than a Venn diagram for presenting data on how beans have grown? Constructing diagrams will help children to see how information combines words with visual elements.

## Reinforcing vocabulary

Reinforcing vocabulary talked about in the literacy hour helps less able children to conceptualise it. Phrases used for writing frames will, for many children, seem strange and unfamiliar, and reinforcement of the same phrases in different contexts will help children to assimilate new language.

## Differentiating subject writing

Children with SEN learn in the same way as children without SEN, but they need more of the same in order to progress in writing and other areas of learning. Access should not lead to over-simplification of subject content. Children with SEN may be supported by further examples to help consolidate new learning, or be helped to generalise what is taught in the literacy hour, and use it in other contexts.

Differentiation by outcome and response may be a leading strategy for subject writing. Now and again, task, content and resources may be adapted, and these could be linked to the current NLS writing objectives to provide further practice in a specific text type.

Group work should reflect what pupils can realistically do. For example, to support work on the Vikings, different groups could:

- write a play based on a Viking raid to support the NLS objective 'to write a playscript' (Year 3, Term 1);
- write questions for other groups to answer based on knowledge gained about the Vikings, with reference to writing questions from NLS Framework Year 1, Term 2;
- generate sentences from a concept keyboard to support the sentence level objectives from Year 1;
- describe a Viking character;
- write a poem in the Viking tradition from having possibly looked at Viking sagas; or
- label artefacts and pictures for the Viking display.

Linking subject writing with the NLS Framework need not always match with the objectives being studied in the same term. If a topic lends itself to specific treatment, there is no reason why the NLS link cannot be backwards as revision of a writing skill, or forwards as advance preparation.

## Extending real communication through writing

Subject work has the potential to develop writing through the communication of views and feelings. The National Writing Project (1989a-d) contains many examples of ways in which writing across subject areas has developed communication. One such example from 'Writing and Learning' (p37-38) describes how a Year 6 class kept maths logs to attempt to dispel fears about maths and to allow pupils to 'scream and shout without making a noise'. About twice a week the class used the last few minutes of the lesson to write in their journals how they felt about the week's maths. Less able children were assured that spellings and handwriting would not be commented on, as the main point of the task was to communicate their views. Figure 9.3 illustrates children's comments.

> Until today, I thought multiplying fractions was easy. Now I realise it isn't. God help me when I do algebra.
>
> I would also want to know if you mark our work like this . . . my capabilitys or my speed or my neatness or all of them. I also get stuck when I have to simplify before multiplying fractions.
>
> I have trouble with some of the large numbers, but when something is to difficult for you and you get it wrong you learn.

**Figure 9.3** Comments from Year 6 pupils' maths logs

The teacher commented on a number of positive points: 'I began to see some of the children . . . in a new light' and 'I learned a great deal from what the children wrote'. The teacher also commented on the 'increasing confidence in the way in which many children handle mathematical language'.

This chapter has focused on the cross-curricular links which enable children to reinforce what is taught in the literacy hour, and to use writing as real communication. Progress, particularly for children with writing difficulties, depends also on effective links between all of the adults involved in raising writing standards. This team approach will be discussed in the following chapter.

*Chapter 10*

# A Team Approach to Success

If writing for all children is to be enhanced using the NLS as its foundation, effective coordination of the different adults involved is essential. This chapter considers the role of three vital support groups: learning support assistants (LSAs); the range of external SEN specialist teachers; and voluntary helpers, e.g. parents and school governors.

## *Why have SEN support?*

Why are support staff so called, and what are they there to do? SEN support exists mainly to comply with the Code of Practice as part of LEA policy for SEN; to support schools' SEN policy and practice; and to enhance the learning of children with SEN in mainstream schools, mainly in literacy and numeracy.

SEN specialists maintain key links between schools and the LEA, and in so doing support the effectiveness of LEA policy for SEN through schools.

## *The literacy team*

All adults perform better if they know how their role works as part of the support plan. Children with SEN often have many adults supporting part of their learning difficulty, and a team approach enables all of the parts to be properly assembled.

Children with SEN assessed at Stages 5 and 3 of the Code are likely to have their difficulties addressed by the class teacher as the key worker; the SENCO as the coordinator; a specialist teacher from a SEN support service; one or more LSAs; and parents, other parent helpers, or governor helpers.

Children with sensory impairments or physical disabilities are likely to have the specialist support of the hearing impaired service (HI), visual impaired service (VI), or physical disability service (PD). Children for whom English is an additional language (EAL), those from a travelling community, and those children with a significant behavioural difficulty (EBD) may also have specialist staff assigned to the literacy team of 'helpers'.

In addition, some schools operate a system whereby sixth form students support children with literacy problems in their feeder primary school; heads and governors also regularly back up SEN support by working with groups of children. All of this is very much to the good.

The range of support can be considerable. Figure 10.1 illustrates possible contributions to a child's literacy support team from different perspectives. The EBD specialist may support writing partly from the perspective of the child's self-esteem and attitudes to literacy, and as part of an Individual Behaviour Plan (IBP).

As a young child, pupil of secondary age, or a student, the learner is the pivot around which support is effective. Without some degree of ownership from learners, support cannot achieve its objectives. Support needs to be coordinated: imagine the confusion for a child on a spelling plan, if staff support the same plan using different methods. While different content and resources are likely to have a positive effect on learning, different, and possibly conflicting, approaches to teaching will only confuse. In this case, too many cooks spoil the broth, only if they are sprinkling into the learning process different ingredients which are unknown to each other. The school and support staff need to work in tandem in order for the specialist contribution to make a difference.

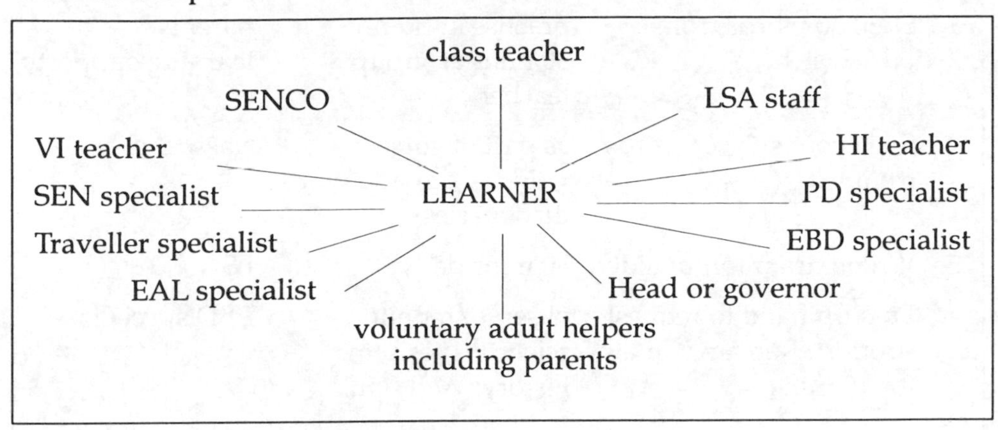


**Figure 10.1** The literacy support team

## The IEP/annual review meeting

IEP review meetings each term, and annual review meetings for Stage 5 pupils, are staging points for assessing progress and planning the next steps. If all adults cannot attend the meetings, it is essential that agreed outcomes are communicated to each member of the team. With the focus on writing, review meetings should reach agreed conclusions on:

- progress on writing targets from the last review;
- the next set of targets for the child to achieve; and
- action to be taken by the literacy team to enable the child to achieve, i.e. who will do what, when and possibly how and where to ensure that identified learning targets are appropriately covered, but without duplication.

Consider a child who has been assessed by the LEA as having significant SpLD, and allocated a statement for SEN. Figure 10.2 identifies possible writing targets, and states the members of the literacy team who could support each one.

| Targets | Strategies | By whom? |
|---|---|---|
| 1. Organise own tools | provide list | class teacher |
| 2. Write dictated sentence with CVC words correct | pair work<br>15 mins daily | LSA |
| 3. Write own sentence with capital letter and full stop | practise at home | parents |
| 4. Spell NLS List 1<br>Spell monosyllabic words with consonant clusters | 30 mins weekly<br>multi-sensory programme | SpLD specialist |

*Teams are to monitor above from a range of writing activities.*

**Figure 10.2** Supporting the writer with SpLD

A child with learning difficulties and behaviour difficulties as illustrated in Figure 10.3 may have different targets, and specialists working with the school to address them.

A child from a travelling family with behavioural difficulties who is considerably behind in writing skills, illustrated in Figure 10.4, will have a different support plan.

| Targets | Strategies | By whom? |
|---|---|---|
| 1. Spell 50 words from NLS List 1 | practise at home<br>30 mins as group teacher | parents<br>learning support |
| 2. Spell core subject words from lists | as part of subject work – provide word dictionaries | class teacher |
| 3. Write paragraph unaided | 30 mins daily | LSA |
| 4. Puts up hand to request support. Remains on task for 10 mins | observe/monitor<br>science: Tues p.m.<br>history: Wed p.m. | EBD specialist |

**Figure 10.3** Supporting learning and behaviour difficulties

| Targets | Strategies | By whom? |
|---|---|---|
| 1. Write three sentences unaided | in-class support during literacy hour Mon/Wed | class teacher<br>specialist from traveller service |
| 2. Write cursive script | 15 mins as pair<br>practise at home | LSA<br>parents |
| 3. Spell 50 NLS words from List 1 | learn to spell word book | learning support teacher |
| 4. Attempt to spell unknown words | segmentation skills | class teacher<br>SENCO |

**Figure 10.4** Combined support for a travelling child

## Supporting medium-term planning

How does the SEN system feed into and reflect NLS planning? The Literacy Coordinator, with key players, is responsible for reading and writing policy, and its reflection into classroom practice. This needs to dovetail with the literacy plan, which in turn links in with the SEN policy. Medium-term planning identifies in what order NLS objectives are transferred to weekly plans:

- how far are children's responses to the previous medium-term plan informing the next one?
- who is involved in medium-term planning?
- are teachers of parallel year groups planning together in order to share resources?
- is information from IEP and annual review meetings fed into medium-term NLS planning?
- is medium-term planning only for literacy hour work, or does it identify catch-up work at the same time?

The medium-term meeting, if attended by relevant support staff, could be a major staging point for literacy planning. The agenda could include:

- planning the next medium-term literacy objectives;
- matching NLS objectives with IEP or annual review targets;
- clarifying SEN support tasks; and
- identifying how catch-up strategies for children with SEN fit in with literacy hour planning.

The meeting could address time-scales and how support staff coordinate input: there are no tried and tested models which fit all schools. Coordinating NLS planning with SEN routines could minimise problems by ensuring efficient use of time.

### Coordinating key players

Where does literacy end and SEN begin? Both the SENCO and the Literacy Coordinator play key roles in writing (and reading) for all. Where involvement overlaps, who takes responsibility for:

- training LSA staff on shared and guided writing?
- training LSA staff on how to address writing difficulties?
- informing parents about the writing policy?
- helping parents of children with SEN to support writing?
- organising parent writing workshops in liaison with the specialist support teacher?
- leading workshops on multi-sensory writing activities?
- organising SEN support staff for writing?

## Learning support assistants (LSAs)

The LSA is a human resource and needs to be projected where it is most needed.

### What is the prime purpose of LSA support?

Is the LSA there to:

- support the classroom in a general sense, e.g. as the other adult during the literacy hour?
- support pupils with statements (funded by the statement)? or
- support groups of pupils at Stage 3 of the Code?

*The LSA in the literacy hour*

The LSA will work more successfully with groups during guided and independent reading and writing if there has been:

- training on the literacy hour and its component parts;
- training on reading and writing skills and strategies;
- training on working with groups; and
- access to the planning process.

During shared reading and writing time, could the LSA:

- assess particular pupils and record their responses?
- prepare resources, e.g. quietly cut up jigsaw cards?
- support access for particular pupils?

Classroom support for children learning English as an additional language has been found particularly useful where the LSA is familiar with Asian languages: Wragg *et al.* (1998) cites the successful role of the LSA as a translator during reading sessions. Easy answers are not to be found but, by exploring options, schools may be helped to find their own solutions from the resources available.

*LSA support for catch-up strategies*

If LSAs are not supporting the hour, are they delivering catch-up lessons? With the focus on writing, is the brief:

- to work on pupils' identified targets from IEPs?
- to help pupils finish work started in the literacy hour?
- to continue with long-term spelling or handwriting plans as part of regular and frequent input?
- to help groups of children finish written work started in subject lessons, but based on NLS objectives?

However they support, we might ensure that LSAs know:
- how their catch-up session fits in and reflects what has been taught in the literacy hour;
- what records are to be kept and stored;
- from whom to request further guidance or the next steps for catch-up work (SEN specialist? SENCO? Class teacher?); and
- the teaching strategies and resources to be used.

### LSA training

If LSAs are to enhance writing skills effectively their training should include:
- interactive group work with writing activities;
- how to include difficult children in group work;
- how to motivate reluctant writers;
- how to use multi-sensory writing approaches, e.g. games;
- how to address spelling difficulties; and
- how to address handwriting difficulties.

Briefing cards (Folens) could assist LSAs in working with literacy and provide useful starting points for training.

## *The SEN external specialist*

Given that priorities for support may have to be made, the following questions may generate debate:
- what is the main purpose of the SEN support?
- is the SEN specialist there to support children with statements, in which case any funding from the statement must be the priority?
- is the SEN support intended for children at Stage 3 of the Code of Practice?
- is the support best used for purposes other than direct teaching of pupils, e.g. training of LSA staff, preparing resources for writing?

If the purpose is to develop literacy, schools need to question, for their particular school, which kind of support will have the most impact: school policy level, classroom level, e.g. supporting class based innovation, or pupil level, by direct involvement with named pupils?

### Team teaching in the literacy hour

If the SEN specialist supports the literacy hour, how can it be fully effective? Teamwork is based on joint awareness of:
- the NLS reading and writing objectives;
- strategies for role sharing in the literacy hour;
- discipline issues – the support teacher needs to know the school behaviour policy;
- how other adult roles in the classroom are to be managed;
- how work, especially writing, is marked and recorded; and
- any pupils to be observed during the hour and by whom.

In general, if the SEN specialist is supporting the literacy hour, pupils' work should relate to the prescribed objectives for that term, with any differentiated stretching. There is little point in supporting a literacy hour unless the SEN specialist and the class teacher observe together the effectiveness of children's learning.

*Performing the support role*

Many of the organisational issues raised in Chapter 7 apply to in-class support work. For example:

- how will the SEN teacher support pupils' independence?
- how do the pupil groupings enable support to work?
- can equipment for sensory-impaired pupils be used?

## Specialist teacher support out of the hour

Again the key question is for what purpose the support is to be used? Support services may support writing by:

- teaching pupils with the worst literacy difficulties;
- helping to organise parent workshops for writing;
- training LSAs on how to address writing difficulties;
- preparing resources for writing, e.g. games and activities, with school staff;
- supporting the SENCO at policy level; and
- supporting assessment of writing and other literacy areas.

Direct teaching could be catch-up work for what has not been grasped in the literacy hour, or preparation work to prime less able pupils for literacy work to follow. In either case, specialist support work should match NLS objectives, broken down into smaller steps as necessary to match IEP targets.

The SEN teacher may design a programme of work, for reading or writing targets, and the strategies and resources used. Figure 10.5 illustrates sample small-step targets.

1. Spells word with first letter correct
   Spells word with first and last letter correct
   Spells first five words from NLS List 1
2. Writes captions for picture – single word
   phrase with adjective/noun
   short sentence

**Figure 10.5** Examples of small-step targets

## The educational psychologist

The role of the educational psychologist (EP) in supporting schools will differ between LEAs. The EP may support writing difficulties by:

- assessment of a pupil's writing skills, commonly to obtain a spelling quotient for LEA assessment;
- contribution to reviews, by report or attendance; or
- contribution to LEA training on writing difficulties, e.g. SpLD or dyspraxia, and training on target-setting.

The EP service may offer advice and guidance, and can often be an untapped well of knowledge on acute writing difficulties. The EP service also works in close liaison with other SEN support specialists.

## Parental and governor support

Parental support is far more likely to be sought for reading than for writing. It may be thought that:

- parents are better able to support reading than writing;
- parents have not the time to be involved with both; and
- helping parents to support reading is less complicated than helping them to support writing.

Priorities need to be set, but parents can support writing without detracting from the focus on reading. Schools need to inform and support parents on all aspects of literacy. The following examples may stimulate ideas:

- inform parents about teaching literacy 'the NLS way'. Include writing as well as reading;
- show parents how reading and writing support each other;
- invite parents to see writing being modelled and shared;
- send home good examples of cross-curricular writing to show parents how writing extends into other subjects;
- show parents of young children how to promote positive attitudes about writing, e.g. by talking about it; and
- involve parents and children together in real writing tasks for the school, e.g. labels for the craft fair, notices.

Reaching all parents is difficult: parents themselves may lack confidence and see themselves as poor writers. The child who says, 'My Dad doesn't do any writing, so I'm not going to,' needs parental support to change that attitude.

## Parents in school

Parents who support in school need to know how the literacy hour works; the school spelling and handwriting approaches used; what the child is working on, e.g. full stops at the end of his sentence; and what records are being kept.

If parents cannot perform their role in school with some degree of independence, their usefulness as an additional adult is lost. An example of the value of parental support for writing comes from the National Writing Project (1989a-d), on responding to and assessing writing. A teacher of Year 3 children found that the initial experience of parents working on writing tasks in the classroom became more valuable as their role changed shape. The teacher comments, 'At first they relied on me to provide . . . subjects for writing. As their confidence grew they began to suggest their own ideas for discussion and writing. My role changed from instigator, to working partner, and eventually to onlooker.'

This teacher goes on to report how the mothers gradually found the confidence to help children develop their own ideas, even if they struggled to put pen to paper. The project culminated in a book for the reception class.

Consistency is crucial. Margerison (1997) stresses that developing literacy for pupils with SEN has ceased to be the role of the 'experts' in SEN: 'It is a partnership between teachers, managers, other professionals, and parents that should be built upon their strengths.' The team model recognises the responsibilities and capabilities of all teachers as a key part of the whole-school literacy team.

*Chapter 11*

# Assessing and Recording Writing

The assessment and recording of writing play an integrated role in the teaching and learning process. This chapter explores ways of assessing and recording writing, with the focus on what works for children with SEN.

## *Assessing and recording writing*

Assessing and recording writing works best in the classroom as part of the teaching context.

### Why assess writing?

Assessment should reveal what children can do and enable teachers to move them on. Often, assessment confirms what children cannot do, and heightens learners' perceptions of their failure. Writing assessment provides information:

- for parents – to inform them of their child's progress;
- for the school – the effectiveness of the writing policy;
- for IEP reviews, i.e. if children have met their targets;
- to analyse trends over time; and
- to support standard assessment tests (SATs) results.

### Principles underpinning writing assessment

Strategies for assessing writing should:

- show progress over time rather than a single snapshot;
- include process pieces as well as final drafts;
- include a range of text types from different subjects;
- involve the writer in assessing his own writing progress;
- indicate writing strengths as well as weaknesses; and
- demonstrate clearly the stage a learner has reached, and what he needs to aim for next.

### Who assesses children's writing?

Writing is often done, placed in a designated place, and marked by the teacher. The NLS approach to literacy emphasises the writer's involvement in the assessment process. If work in process as well as final drafts is to count towards a rounded picture of what children can do, assessment needs to be with the writer. Children's ownership of their writing to some degree is part of their developing independence. Assessment could have a range of assessors, including:

- the reader for whom the written work is intended;
- other teachers, i.e. reading written work between classes;
- LSAs;
- parents – as part of their training in what to look for; and
- other children.

Involving parents in assessment may help to develop their interest and their skills in working with children on writing, and could include:

- talking to them about their child's writing;
- asking their views on a piece of writing and skilfully developing the conversation around writing skills;
- holding meetings now and again to discuss common writing difficulties, at which parent representatives are invited.

The National Writing Project (1989a-d) emphasised the central role of the reader as an assessor of what is written. Children are more likely to develop healthy attitudes to writing if they are involved in assessing the writing of others. The project included all ages of child involvement. From a six-year-old, 'I liked the Bitt when you fell over and I liked it when you buried the wolf. Becose it was funny . . .'

The project reminds all those involved in developing children's writing that, 'a child . . . who can discuss another child's writing . . . is more likely to become a critical and reflective writer than the child accustomed to receiving only a teacher's response'.

## How is writing assessed?

If process is to feature as well as the final product then assessment includes the planning and discussion stages as well as the writing itself. Assessment could involve:

- observing children writing alone;
- observing children's writing activities with others;
- listening to children talking about their writing;
- reading their writing logs, and 'own choice' books;
- analysing children's 'try-it-first' spelling books;
- observing group discussion at the planning stage;
- asking open or closed questions about writing;
- appraising children's writing efforts;
- traditional marking strategies;
- discussing achievements, e.g. the writing conference; or
- posing writing problems for pupils and analysing solutions.

Recording what is observed need not be time-consuming: an exercise book with dated comments as illustrated in Figure 11.1 should do.

### *Marking writing*

Marking often highlights what is wrong, overshadowing what is right. 'Responding' to writing may be a more effective means of assessing, and feeding back to the writer. Responses can be:

- written – as comments on the paper;
- oral – through discussion; or
- demonstrative – as a smile, frown or gesture.

Responses to written work may be personal or collaborative – Figure 11.2 questions a range of responses to written work.

Responses depend on the content of the writing; anything confidential would not be aired at an IEP review meeting. Alternatively, a response to writing would not cause embarrassment for a child in front of the class. Responses to writing could represent common writing problems, e.g. full stops, and involve an oral response to an ability group on punctuation, with a written response in the child's book, e.g. with reference to mis-spelt words only? Sensitive responses to writing promote a more relaxing writing environment.

| Continuous writing observation record | |
|---|---|
| Name A Jones Class 4H Year 4 School Whitefield | |
| **Date** | **Skills and strategies observed** |
| 13/1/98 | wrote poem unaided — free form — improved confidence |
| 16/1 | wrote own questions during guided writing session |
| 28/1 | attempted own spellings in geography — vowels poor |
| 16/2 | used writing frame to write persuasive piece — full stops largely correct |
| 10/3 | most high frequency words correct |
| 17/3 | chose to work on letter with Jane A. |
| 19/3 | looked up 'Saturday' in reference area |
| 23/3 | worked on group notice for jumble sale |
| **Next steps for IEP**<br>• cont' to encourage unaided writing<br>• identify spellings to be focused on<br>• cont' to encourage voluntary writing<br>• increase independence | |

**Figure 11.1** Observing and recording writing

| **Written** | **Oral** | **Demonstrative** |
|---|---|---|
| What is written? | To the child only? | In what form? |
| Where? | To an ability group? | For what value? |
| When? | To whole class? | As a reward? |
| Personal or collaborative?<br>To parent only? To child only? To another teacher?<br>To child and parent together? To whole class?<br>To all staff during assessment moderation session?<br>To all members of an IEP review meeting? | | |

**Figure 11.2** Responses to written work

A final point on responding to writing refers back to the National Writing Project (1989a d), and comes from children themselves, reported through their teacher, 'They said — although they'd all like to have "good", they would like to know why it was good — what part of it . . . when I asked why, they said because it would tell you which things to do next time.'

### *Assessing particular forms of difficulty*

If learners have a particular difficulty with writing which may be affected by a cultural, medical or a social problem, specialist advice should be sought. Assessment for learners with dyspraxia will ascertain how writing is affected and what programme needs to address it. Similarly, assessment for a child with symptoms of SpLD needs a specialist. Children with SpLD can only be helped if their problems are identified in time for them to benefit from programmes put in place to address them.

Assessing children learning English as an additional language is fraught with problems. The 1993 Education Act (revised in 1996), stated clearly that, 'A child must not be taken as having a learning difficulty, solely because the language ... in which he is ... taught is different from a language ... spoken in his home' (Section 159). Yet the Code of Practice (DfE 1994) stresses early identification of SEN. Identifying bilingual pupils with SEN may involve mother-tongue assessment. Guidelines for establishing the distinction between language difficulties and SEN are published by Oldham Education and Leisure, through their Ethnic Minorities Support Service (1998).

## A staged model for assessment and recording

The three stage model, in Figure 11.3, suggests how elements of assessment can be organised into a manageable time-scale.

| Assessment | Purpose and context |
|---|---|
| 1. Continuous | continuous collection of data<br>from range of sources and contexts<br>to inform short-term planning |
| 2. Cumulative | termly (or half-termly) collation of data<br>analysis of teaching and learning<br>informs medium-term planning |
| 3. Summative | annual summary using continuous and cumulative documentation<br>for transition between years/stages<br>for reporting to parents<br>evaluates writing achievement patterns |

**Figure 11.3** Staged model for assessing and recording writing

### Continuous assessment and recording

There are valid reasons why all children should have learning targets; these could be for groups as well as individuals. Pupil targets promote ownership of learning, which lead to and reflect independence, stimulate the learning process, and enable teaching to be manageable and enjoyable.

*Involving learners in assessing and recording*

How far can children be assessors and recorders in a way that is meaningful as well as manageable? Answers depend partly on expectations, and how much weight is placed on training all pupils to accept some responsibility for their learning. If the literacy hour is to raise literacy standards, the traditional assessment model may have to be questioned.

*Self-assessing handwriting*

Once children have left the stage of letter formation, and are on their way through the handwriting process, a self-assessment checklist, as shown in Figure 11.4, could help them to maintain the required standards. Use of the word 'my' helps to make the checklist more personal to the writer.

*Self-assessing spelling*

If learners are to assess their own spellings they must know what to look for. Personal targets may have identified:

- which common, high-frequency spellings are already 'known' and are expected to be right;
- which phonic clusters or vowel digraphs are part of the learners' knowledge, or are currently being worked on; or
- what particular problems the learner is to avoid.

| Handwriting checklist | | |
|---|---|---|
| **Name** . . . . . . . . . . **Class** . . . . . . . . . **Date** . . . . . . . . . | | |
| *Look carefully at your handwriting.* | | |
| *Answer the questions.* | **YES** | **NO** |
| Are my letters neatly formed? | | |
| Can my teacher and friends read it? | | |
| Is each letter the same size? | | |
| Are there spaces between my words? | | |
| Is my writing joined if it needs to be? | | |
| Have I used capital letters correctly? | | |
| *Attach your writing sample to this checklist. Put your name on both. Put it in the box marked 'Assessment'.* | | |

**Figure 11.4** Handwriting checklist

As part of a child's spelling plan, a checklist for spellings would focus only on those words the child can identify. If he could identify all wrong spellings he would not have a spelling problem. A checklist could be placed in the child's book with a reminder of the particular groups of words to be focused on. Even children with severe spelling problems need to be taught how to combat their difficulty. Placing reminders of common spelling errors on a chart or in a child's book helps them gradually to focus in on them, e.g. 'there' and 'their', or 'too', 'to' and 'two'.

Using a spell-checker is unhelpful at the early stages as the device finds the nearest version of the 'word'. If the child's spelling is bizarre the spell-checker will produce a word which makes no sense at all in the child's writing.

### *Self-assessing at text level*

Children with SEN find it difficult to assess any part of their writing if too much is expected at once. If spellings or handwriting can be assessed at separate readings, there may be a better chance of learners picking up errors at whole text level. Children should be asking:

- do my sentences make sense?
- are any words missed out?
- is my punctuation correct?
- have I used some words too often (repetition)?
- do my sentences have different beginnings?
- are my sentences different lengths, with some long and some short?
- could my nouns and verbs be stronger?
- do my paragraphs stick to one main idea?
- does my writing have an opening, a strong middle and a clear ending (fiction and non-fiction)?

### *Working as response partners*

It may take time for children with learning difficulties to do this properly, but the results are well worth the initial time and effort. In pairs or small groups, children assess each other's writing and talk about it afterwards. A marking chart is useful. This could simply be:

- putting a wavy line under a suspect spelling;
- circling a suspect item of punctuation;
- highlighting a sentence which may need reworking;
- underlining a particular word which could be stronger; or
- placing a 'P' beside where a fresh paragraph might begin.

Following the text-marking, children talk about each mark. Depending on the discussion, the writer amends it or not. The marking chart needs to be tailored to the needs of particular ability levels, so that response partner work reflects any individual self-assessment strategies being used.

Response partner work does not replace self-assessment, but both strategies help less able writers to assess their writing more effectively. Ground rules may include:

- always respect each other's work;
- never be unkind to your partner;
- positive criticism says what is good as well as what could be better; and
- the writer makes the final decision on his own piece.

### *A customised writing checklist*

The self-assessment list in Figure 11.5 was placed into a child's book as a reminder of his own common writing errors. Errors no longer evident are crossed off the list, and form a comforting reminder of progress for the learner.

**My own writing checklist**

**Name** John B **Year** 3 **Date started** April 5th '97

I have put a full stop at the end of my sentence.

~~The words from my Spelling List 1 are right.~~ ✓

I have not put a capital B in the middle of words.

I have not written 'and' too many times.

I have not mixed up the 'I' and 'he' ways of writing (1st and 3rd person).

**Figure 11.5** A customised writing checklist

Self-assessment checklists used appropriately, with care, and taking into account the maturity of the writer, help to stimulate writing ownership for all learners.

### *The Record Of Achievement (ROA)*

> A record of achievement is a cumulative record of an individual child's all round achievement. It records positive achievements and ideally involves children, teachers and parents in the process of its production. (DES 1990)

The ROA asks, 'How well am I doing?' and encourages children, with adult support, to evaluate and make decisions about their writing progress. In order for the ROA not to become a random and overloaded file, selection is necessary. The following could be filed in the ROA:

- selected samples of the range of text types;
- positive comments from teachers, parents and others;
- examples of writing certificates;
- self-assessment writing checklists;
- evidence of process work that demonstrates a significant leap forward, with their final drafts;
- a copy of the writing conference record (later section); and
- comments and notes on tests performed well.

Entries for the ROA need to be discussed by pupil and teacher, dated and filed chronologically, and where necessary commented on, e.g. why was the piece selected and what makes it good enough? The purpose of an ROA is to represent a child's personal best, and to record progress over time. Self-assessment asks, 'How am I doing?' as well as 'How many have I got right?' It is qualitative as well as quantitative.

*Collecting data*

Data soon mounts up and needs to form part of a literacy assessment system, parts of which can be retrieved as needed (e.g. for IEP review meetings, parents' evenings etc.). Data from ongoing assessment and recording feeds cumulative assessment and could also include:

- pupils' 'own choice' books;
- pupils' logs, e.g. a maths log;
- teacher comments from observations;
- parents' comments on work done at home or at school;
- LSA records; and
- SEN specialist records which feed cumulative assessment meetings, i.e. reports for IEP and annual review meetings.

## Cumulative assessment and recording

Cumulative assessment analyses work done during the previous term, or half-term if time allows, and reflects three main contexts for assessing writing progress.

*The writing conference*

Although writing discussion with pupils is ongoing, time may not allow for cumulative, in-depth discussion more than once or twice a term. A longer session offers additional time to address the questions, 'How well am I doing? and 'What am I reaching for next?'

Figure 11.6 provides part of the discussion with Mark, aged nine, based upon the text shown. Figure 11.7 records the outcome of Mark's writing conference and the targets set for the next term.

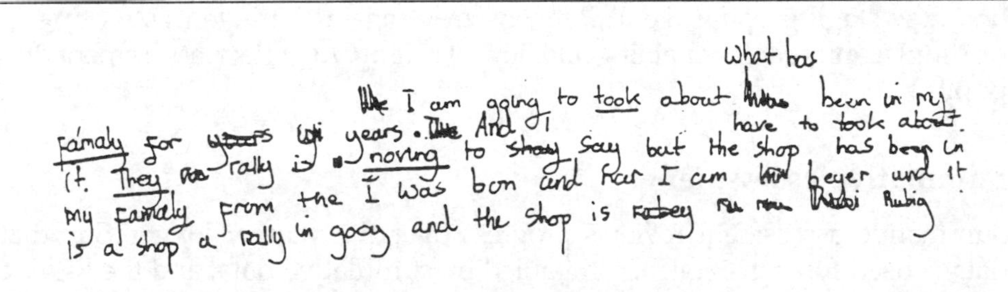

After having read the piece of writing, the conversation went something like:
Mr T: Let's see how we can improve it. What do you think?
Mark: It's untidy . . . I've done a lot of crossings out.
Mr T: Good. If you've crossed out, it shows you've thought about it. Nobody gets it right first time. What do you think we need to focus on?
Mark: My spellings . . . I think . . . and my words get mixed up.
Mr T: How do you think we can crack it?
Mark: I don't know . . .
Mr T: Let's look at the words I've underlined. To start with, suppose we work on these? That'll help. Don't forget, you've got a lot of them right.
Mark: Okay.

**Figure 11.6** Part of Mark's writing conference discussion

Writing (or reading) conferencing could be worked from a rota system, using one or two timetabled afternoons as conference time. While this is happening, children could be working on unfinished writing from the week, or activities which require no adult input.

| Writing conference outcome | Name Mark P | Date 13/6 |
|---|---|---|
| **Spelling targets** | **Strategies** | **IEP link** |
| 1. Reinforce high-frequency words | Mark to self-check Teacher monitor it | class teacher and LSA |
| 2. Use analogy to spell families of words | 15 mins with LSA monitor in literacy hour | link with LSA work on spellings |
| 3. Spell common words beginning with 'the' (they, then, there) | focused work on blue group in literacy hour | group time with SENCO |

**Figure 11.7** Part of Mark's conference outcome

*IEP review meeting*

The IEP review meeting accumulates progress reports from all professionals and parents involved with a child and should represent a summary of continuous assessment over the term. Evidence from the ROA, showing selected examples of writing, could be useful at this meeting. It is important for the learner and his parents to be fully involved, and that the question, 'What am I reaching for next?' is answered in terms of the next learning targets.

*NLS medium-term planning*

The assessment suggestions made so far in this chapter have drawn on previous good classroom practice for use in the uncharted waters of the NLS and the literacy hour. Assessment needs to be shared: medium-term planning could map onto key staging points, i.e. IEP review meetings and the term's writing (plus reading) conferences, enabling literacy planning to reflect assessment for all pupils.

### Summative assessment

Summative assessment reviews progress over the year or longer. Summative data is used for transition, accompanied by cumulative data, and the ROA, and should follow the child into the next year, key stage, secondary school, or to or from a special school. Summative assessment for writing might include annual spelling tests and Key Stage SATs results.

*National feedback on writing*

The Qualifications and Curriculum Authority (1998) has published national feedback on the results of 1997 National Curriculum Assessments. Key features of performance across key stages indicated, among other interesting trends, that, 'more children choose to write narrative than non-narrative . . . children need help with how to organise informative and discursive texts'. This feedback provides invaluable summative assessment to inform schools' writing policy.

## Reporting to parents (and children)

If communication with parents has been a two-way process, the annual report presents no surprises. Parents will have been informed of any writing difficulties and should have responded to the school's efforts to address them together. Similarly, if continuous and cumulative assessment strategies and records have featured throughout the year, the content of the parental report almost writes itself. Parental reports on literacy progress are more likely to reach their readership if they are:

- specific – stating what a child can, and cannot, do;
- projected – stating the next stages of learning; and
- reader-friendly – written for parents to understand.

Reports may encourage more parents to address writing difficulties if they offer suggestions for how parents can support writing.

The assessment and planning cycle is not a complete jigsaw; all classroom pieces rarely fit together to produce a perfect picture. Continuous assessment and recording which feeds a cumulative, and summative, system will benefit all pupils and teachers.

# Conclusion

This book has focused on writing as part of literacy, through the National Literacy Strategy objectives for word, sentence and text level work, which include all primary age children. A key theme throughout has been the integration of writing skills and strategies through their whole context, with due regard to cross-curricular writing.

Teamwork is the key to success. The thought-provoking words of Maria Landy, from a conference on SEN and the literacy hour, capture the essence of raising writing standards for all:

**T** – together
**E** – everyone
**A** – achieves
**M** – more.

# Bibliography


Addy, L. M. (1998) *Perceptuo Motor Disorders: Identification and Remediation*. York: University of Ripon and York St John.

Alston, J. (1995) *Assessing and Promoting Writing Skills*. Tamworth: NASEN.

Baker, A. (1995) 'Real writing, real writers: a question of choice', in Raban, B. (ed.) *Practical Ways to Teach Writing*. Ward Lock International.

Attwood, T. (1994) *Dyslexia in Schools – A Guide for all Teachers*. First and Best Education.

Bentley, D. (1998) *Helping Struggling Writers*, paper presented at a lecture at Wynyard Hall SEN Exhibition.

Browne, A. (1996) *Developing Language and Literacy, 3-8*. London: Paul Chapman Publishing.

Bullock Report (1975) *A Language for Life*. London: HMSO.

Depree, H. and Iverson, S. (1994) *Early Literacy in the Classroom*. New Zealand: Lands End Publishing.

DES (1990) Circular 8/90.

DfE (1994) *The Code of Practice for the Identification and Assessment of Special Educational Needs*. London: HMSO.

DfE (1995) *English in the National Curriculum*. London: HMSO.

DfEE (1998) *National Literacy Strategy: Framework for Teaching*. London: HMSO.

Ethnic Minorities Support Service (1998) *Guidelines for the Assessment of Bilingual Pupils who may have Learning Difficulties*. Centre for Professional Development, Rosary Road, Fitton Hill, Oldham OL8 2QE.

Gentry, J. R. (1987) *SPEL . . . is a four letter word*. Leamington Spa: Scholastic Publications.

Gorman, T., and Brooks, G. (1996) *Assessing Young Children's Writing*. London: Basic Skills Agency.

Hodgson, M. (1995) *Show Them How to Write*. New Zealand: Lands End Publishing.

Hoffman, M. (1976) *Reading, Writing and Relevance*. London: Hodder and Stoughton.

Iverson, S. (1997) *A Blueprint for Literacy Success*. London: Kingscourt Publishing.

Iverson, S. and Reeder, T. (1998) *Organizing for a Literacy Hour*. London: Kingscourt Publishing.

Jarman, C. (1979) *The Development of Handwriting Skills*. Oxford: Basil Blackwell Publishers.

Lewis, M. and Wray, D. (1996) *Writing Frames*. Reading: University of Reading.

Lewis, M. and Wray, D. (1998) *Writing Across the Curriculum*. Reading: University of Reading.

Malone, G. and Smith, D. (1996) *Learning to Learn*. Tamworth: NASEN.

Margerison, A. (1997), 'Class teachers and the role of classroom assistants in the delivery of special educational needs', *Support for Learning* **12**(4).

National Writing Project (1989a) *Audiences for Writing*. Walton-on-Thames: Thomas Nelson and Sons.

National Writing Project (1989b) *Becoming a Writer*. Walton-on-Thames: Thomas Nelson and Sons.

National Writing Project (1989c) *Responding to and Assessing Writing*. Walton-on-Thames: Thomas Nelson and Sons.

National Writing Project (1989d) *Writing and Learning*. Walton-on-Thames: Thomas Nelson and Sons.

Qualifications and Curriculum Assessment Authority (1998) *Report on the National Curriculum Assessments for 7-year-olds*. London: QCA.

Redfern, A. (1993) *Practical Ways to Teach Spelling*. Reading: University of Reading.

Redfern, A. and Edwards, V. (1997) *Practical Ways to Inspire Young Authors*. Reading: University of Reading.

Rees, F. (1996) *The Writing Repertoire: Developing Writing at Key Stage 2*. Slough: National Foundation for Educational Research.

Sassoon, R. (1991) *Handwriting: The Way to Teach it*. Cheltenham: Stanley Thornes.

School Curriculum and Assessment Authority (1995) *Consistency in Teacher Assessment – Exemplification of Standards*.London: SCAA Publications.

Smith, D. (1996) *Specific Learning Difficulties*. Tamworth: NASEN.

Wragg, E. C., Wragg, C. M., Haynes, G. S. and Chamberlain, R. P. (1998) *Improving Literacy in the Primary School*. London: Routledge.

# Useful Addresses

Basic Skills Agency, Commonwealth House, 1-19 New Oxford Street, London, WC1A 1NU
Easylearn, Trent House, Fiskerton, Southwell, Nottinghamshire, NG25 0UH
Folens Publishers Ltd, Albert House, Apex Business Park, Boscombe Road, Dunstable, Beds, LU5 4RL
GAMZ, 25 Albert Park Road, Malvern, Worcestershire, WR14 1HW
H.E.L.P. Educational Games, 29 Churchill Close, Didcot, Oxon, OX11 7BX
Jolly Phonics, Tailours House, High Road, Chigwell, Essex, IG7 6DL
LDA/NES Arnold, Ludlow Hill Road, West Bridgford, Nottingham, NG2 6HD
Learning Materials Ltd, Dixon Street, Wolverhampton, WV2 2BX
Letterland Ltd, Barton, Cambridge, CB3 7AY
PAT Publications, Educational Psychology Service, County Hall, Aylesbury, Bucks, HP20 1UZ
REM Special Needs Catalogue for ICT, Great Western House, Langport, Somerset, TA10 9YU
Rhyme World, Heinemann Educational, Freepost, PO Box 970, Oxford, OX2 8BR
Special Needs Learning Materials, Sheffield Hallam University Press, Adsetts Centre, City Campus, Sheffield, S1 1WB
Units of Sound, The Dyslexia Institute, 133 Gresham Road, Staines, Middlesex, TW18 2AJ
Word Shark, White Space, 41 Mall Road, London, W6 9DG

# Index